Max Pemberton

The Little Huguenot
A Romance of Fountainebleau

ISBN/EAN: 9783744694148

Printed in Europe, USA, Canada, Australia, Japan

Cover: Foto ©Thomas Meinert / pixelio.de

More available books at **www.hansebooks.com**

"THE LITTLE HUGUENOT"

𝕬 𝕽𝖔𝖒𝖆𝖓𝖈𝖊 𝖔𝖋 𝕱𝖔𝖓𝖙𝖆𝖎𝖓𝖊𝖇𝖑𝖊𝖆𝖚

BY

MAX PEMBERTON

AUTHOR OF "THE IMPREGNABLE CITY," ETC

———

NEW YORK

DODD, MEAD & COMPANY

1895

CONTENTS.

CHAPTER I.

PAGE

PEPIN IS BLESSED............................ 7

CHAPTER II.

AT THE GATE OF THE CHÂTEAU............ 19

CHAPTER III.

GABRIELLE DE VERNET..................... 26

CHAPTER IV.

THE KINGFISHER AND THE CROWS......... 37

CHAPTER V.

THE ABBÉ GONDY COUNTS HIS SPOONS.... 49

CHAPTER VI.

IN THE BOWER OF VIOLETS.............. 57

CHAPTER VII.

THE ABBÉ GONDY WRITES A SERMON 70

5

Contents.

CHAPTER VIII.

PAGE

Masking in the Woods.............. 82

CHAPTER IX.

Pepin Makes a Bargain.............. 99

CHAPTER X.

The Woman and the Priest.......... 107

CHAPTER XI.

The Abbé and the Tree............. 122

CHAPTER XII.

De Guyon Hears the News.......... 133

CHAPTER XIII.

The Apparition.................... 143

CHAPTER XIV.

The King Sups.................... 159

CHAPTER XV.

Exodus.... 171

"The Little Huguenot."

CHAPTER I.

PEPIN IS BLESSED.

THE priest had a volume of Cicero
upon his lap, and in his right hand
there was a rosary carved of amber
and of gold.   Though the sun's beams
fell soft in the glen, and the grass was
green and rich, and a canopy of young
leaves cast welcome shade upon his
face, he continued to read the oration
upon which his eyes had fallen, and
to banish those seductive whisperings
of the devil, that he should lay himself down and sleep.   Insensible to
the wooing music of the gushing cas-
cade, or to that stillness which had
come upon all nature as the heat of

the day fell, he maintained a fine rigidity of posture as he sat upright upon a boulder of stone, and bent his whole soul to the study of the black-lettered text before him. Hours passed and found his attitude unchanged ; a distant church bell chimed the quarters dolefully, and drew from him no other response than the mutter of an *Ave;* the shadows in the glen lengthened and lengthened ; even the first freshness of night breathed upon the forest, and left him insensible to all but those problems of his faith which crowded upon his mind.

Death and sleep and eternity ! A priest may think even of these. Six years before this year, 1772, Père Cavaignac was far too busy snatching souls in Paris to trouble himself with those more subtle reasonings to which a new philosophy had turned. But here in the depths of the forest of Fontainebleau, it was otherwise. The very atmosphere seemed dream-giving and full of spells. The unbroken silence of the thickets, the music of

8

the glittering falls, the dark places of pools and caverns, threw back the man's mind upon itself, and wrung from him the question, To what end? Why was he an exile from the capital? Why was his home a hut of logs hidden even from the eyes of the woodlanders? For what cause did he eat black bread and drink sour wine? That he might sleep for ever after death as he had slept through eternity before his birth? Night and the new philosophy told him that here was his answer ; day and the soul's voice rekindled his faith so that he seemed to behold the Christ walking in the forest before him. And in these moments, the remembrance that he was a hunted man, that when next he looked upon the city that he loved it would be for the last time, exalted his whole being, and lifted him up in visions to the gates of heaven itself.

Night began to come down in earnest when at last the Jesuit closed his book. He had sat so still in his

meditation that a deer thrust herself
through the bracken not fifty yards
from him, and drank undisturbed at
the rippling brook.   A great eagle
was soaring high above him ; and oft
as he listened he could hear the crafty
patter of a wolf or the screech of a
heron in the distant marsh.   There
was no tongue of the forest with
which six years of exile had not made
him familiar ; no note of bird or
beast that was novel enough to carry
his mind from the path it followed.
From man alone he turned, hiding
himself in the very depths of the brack-
en, frequenting the darker caves, lurk-
ing in the glens where the springs bub-
bled and the adder sunned himself.
It was not alone that the edict of ban-
ishment which had fallen upon his
Order made men a danger to him.
He had been indiscreet enough to believe that the broad principles of his
faith were meant to bind prince and
peasant alike ; and he had even de-
nounced the profligacy of kings from
the pulpit ; and this with so fanatical

a zeal that men cried, " Here is a
new Ravaillac—let his Majesty beware of him !" From that day there
was no den dark enough to hide him
in Paris, no friend so powerful that
he could find shelter in his house.
He fled to the forest, and lurked there
waiting and watching, as his rector
had commanded him.

The deer drank at the stream, and
bounded into the thicket again ; the
silver birches swayed their branches
before the gentle west wind ; a clock
in the distant village chimed the hour
of seven. The priest rose from his
seat, and wrapped himself in the
warm black cape which served him
for cloak by day and blanket by
night. Then he forced his way
through the bushes and struck upon
a narrow, bramble-hidden path which
carried him out upon the lawn-like
sward above. Here were great
gnarled oaks and groves of yoke-
elms ; undulating sweeps of the finest
grass land all carpeted with violets ;
pools deep down in the shady glades ;

even beaches of the finest yellow sand, where the brooklets made music in their pebbly beds. But the Jesuit had eyes for none of these things. He stood at the glen's head, motionless, irresolute, perhaps even fearful. A small company of mounted men had debouched from the opposite wood ; and seeing him, one of their number set spurs to the beast he rode and galloped furiously across the grass.

The man was ill-dressed, and odd enough to be remarkable anywhere. He wore a leather jerkin about his body, and a broad-brimmed hat with the stump of a feather in it. His calves were bound round with strips of bright green cloth, and his breeches were balloon-shaped and of prodigious size. He had a pair of little twinkling eyes which danced like the flame of a candle in the wind, and his cheeks were so fat that rolls of flesh almost hid his mouth. For sword he carried a cudgel of black wood ; and from the holster, where his pistols should have been, the end of a four-holed flageolet protruded. But conspicuous among his accoutrements was a wine-skin with little in it, and this he held his hand upon lovingly while he addressed the Jesuit.

"Holy Mother of God, defend me from all devils!" said he, surveying the motionless priest with some curiosity; and then, in quick correction, he added:

"Thy blessing, my father!"

The Jesuit turned upon him a swift, searching glance.

"What do you want with me?" he asked in a hard, cold, rarely used voice.

"No other service than one of charity, most reverend sir. I am a man of peace, as you may observe, carrying no other weapon than that which may rob men of their feet—to wit, may set them to the dance, the ballad, the pasquil and those light enjoyments of the flesh which our master Horace has even deigned to

13

commend on occasion. And now for
my sins, for which I pray the inter-
cession of my holy patron, whose
honourable name I happen to have
forgotten, I—who know the forest
better than the Mass book—am lost
in this tangle at a moment when the
natural humour of man leads him to
meat and even to a cup of wine.
Take me to these, my father, and I
will jingle so many silver pieces in
your hand that a whole legion of
souls shall to-morrow go dancing out
of purgatory."

The man stopped for want of
breath. The priest was about to
plunge again into the thicket, leaving
him unanswered, when the others of
the cavalcade rode up, and the leader,
who was dressed in the uniform of
the king's musketeers, reined in his
horse and doffed his plumed hat to
the ecclesiastic.

"Sir," said he, "I am a lieutenant
of the guard bound upon a mission
from his Majesty to the Château aux
Loups, which, as you may be aware,

is the residence of Madame La Comtesse de Vernet. If you can set us on the way thither——"

"Or to any decent inn where we may find food and drink," chimed in the first fellow.

"Pepin, keep your tongue still."

"Nay, my captain, there is no hand in France strong enough to hold it."

"If you can set us, I say, on the road thither," continued the other, ignoring his servant, and addressing the Jesuit, "I will see that we do not forget the service."

The priest had looked up quickly at the mention of the Château aux Loups. For a moment he seemed to be occupied counting the number of the escort, and this the leader of it observed.

"Fear nothing from these men, sir," said he, "my mission is an honourable one, and will be welcome to the countess. By the Mass, she should be glad of a little company in such a wilderness as this."

"Your mission is an honourable
one—and yet you come from the
king, sir?" said the priest now looking the lieutenant full in the face.

"Aye, honourable, indeed," inter-
rupted the buffoon, Pepin; "and
hark ye, my father, another word
such as that and I will even lay my
cudgel on your back. The devil take
you for a loutish brawler. I would
as soon talk with a throaty Spaniard."

"Pepin, if you do not keep your
tongue still, I will cut it out," said
the Lieutenant de Guyon, turning
round lazily in his saddle.

"Aye, my master, that would be a
service, for on my life it is as dry as
a peppercorn."

The priest had seemed to be thinking deeply while servant and master
thus disputed. In truth, a hundred
questions were troubling him. Why
had de Guyon, a notorious tool of du
Barry, come with an escort of six
musketeers and this clown to the retreat of Gabrielle de Vernet? What
evil did the visit portend? Of what

meaning was it to him personally—
or to his Order, which had found in
the girlish mistress of the château one
of its sincerest friends ? Before he
could answer any single suggestion,
the captain of the band spoke again.

"I am awaiting your answer, my father. You have heard of madame?"

The priest answered slowly.

"So surely have I heard of her,
and of the holy way she walks, that
if I thought you had come here meaning any ill to her, I would strike you
down with my own hand. Paul de
Guyon, look where you go, lest you
lose the path and your eyes be blinded. You talk to me of an honourable
mission, but what of honour hath the
king with Gabrielle de Vernet?
Speak no lies lest the Almighty God
blast them on your lips."

He stood with arm outstretched
and fire in his eyes, and for a moment
the other quailed before him ; but de
Guyon recovered himself quickly,
and cloaking his anger as he might,
he gave rein to his horse.

"Did our time not press, master priest," said he, "I would pause awhile to knock sense into your head with the flat of my sword. A curse on you and your warnings, too. We will even find the château for ourselves."

He turned away making a sign to his men ; but the buffoon bent down from his saddle and placed a hand upon the priest's shoulder.

"Benedicite ! holy father," said he, "but you are free with your warnings. And hark ye, I, Pepin the fool, have a word of warning also. Get to your hut, François Cavaignac, for I recognise you, and by the blessed Host I will have you hanged as high as yonder elm."

The priest's hand trembled for a moment upon the hilt of the dagger which his cassock concealed. But it was only for a moment. Conquering his temper, and disdaining other weapon than his fist, he suddenly dealt the jester a rousing box on the ear, and then plunged into the thicket.

CHAPTER II.

PEPIN rubbed his ear ruefully, and sat looking at the bushes wherein the priest had disappeared.

" Dog of a Jesuit," he muttered, " if you had stayed——"

He made an ugly grimace with the words, and finished what wine there was in the skin.   Then, remembering that the others had now ridden out of hearing, he set spurs to his mule and galloped after them.

" So the priest boxed your ears ?" said de Guyon, surveying him with some amusement.

" *Parbleu!* Excellency, he did but give me his benediction."

" I wish he had knocked some sense into your head."

" Would you cry ' A miracle ! ' *mon maître ?*"

19

" I would cry anything you please
if it would set me on the road again.
I thought you knew every path in the
forest. You told me so when I engaged you at the Barrière d'Enfer."

" Aye, and that is so, sir. Every
path I know, and yet which path is
which, the devil take me if I can say.
Look yonder now ; there is a grove
of yoke-elms with a wood of pines
beyond it, and a brook hollow be-
twixt and between. I could name a
hundred such within ten leagues from
the Table du Roi. Oh, truly, *mon
maître*, I know the forest as a horse
knows the stable."

De Guyon, whose beast stumbled
often upon the sandy track, and
whose patience was fast ebbing, answered him with a fresh objurgation
—long and lasting. It was now near
to being full dark, and but for the
light of the moonbeams, which fell
soft upon copse and thicket and
seemed to cast a snowy mantle—so
white it was—upon every leaf and
bush, the way would have been im-

possible.   Yet the scene was one of
exceeding beauty.   The shiver of the
aspen, the ripple of brook or stream,
the long-drawn note of a night bird
intensified the dreamy silence of the
forest.   Here and there when a horse
forced his way through the bramble
with a snap of twigs and a rustle of
boughs, a wolf sprang out of his cover
and raced across the sward.   The
shimmer of the light in many a glade
showed stags browsing, or wild ponies
herding.   But of habitation there was
no sign, nor of man.

The little troop must have left the
priest twenty minutes before de
Guyon resumed his conversation with
the rogue who had led him on such a
fool's errand.   The stillness of the
forest and the spell of the night,
wedded to his fatigue, had quelled
the words upon his lips, and com-
pelled him to remember upon what
emprise he was embarked.   He began to wonder by what manner of
cunning and tale he should lead
" the little Huguenot," Gabrielle de

Vernet, from her nest in the forest to the intrigues and dangers of the palace. He asked himself if all the stories of her wit and beauty were the mere fancies of her friends, or pretty realities which he must know and cope with. He remembered that he had met her once at Paris in the house of her cousin Claude Vernet, the painter; but that was two years ago, immediately after the death of her husband, Comte de Vernet, the uncompromising foe to the Catholic faith, and before she withdrew to the château to put into practice a creed built on the confession of the Savoyard Vicar, added to a certain orthodoxy which satisfied her fat kinsman, the Abbé Gondy, who regarded her possessions with the eyes of a father and a devout son of the Holy Church. The lieutenant could recall nothing of her features; he knew nothing of her life but such facts as were told in the gossip of the ramparts and the salon. Nor did he hold it possible that she would offer any objection to

accompany him to the palace—there
to set her views and opinions before
his Majesty. Her views and opinions! What a play it was! And
how the king would listen to the
creed of such a piquant disciple!
What a task the conversion would
be. He began even to wonder who
would marry her when the royal ears
were weary of her platitudes, and the
spell of debauchery had chilled her
zeal.

With such thoughts for company,
he rode on in silence. They had
now come out upon park-like land,
where great oaks cast black rings of
shade ; and a lake, harbouring many
wild-fowl, shone like a mirror of silver. There was a great wood, black
and seemingly impenetrable, upon
the far shore of the lake, and when
de Guyon observed this, he drew
rein and surveyed his environment.

" Well, rogue," said he to Pepin,
" where have you brought us now ?"

" By the blood of John, that's what
I begin to ask myself."

De Guyon looked at him for a moment with withering contempt in his glance.

"Unspeakable fool," said he, "I have the mind to box your ears as the priest did."

"Aye, that would be something ; but look you, my master, a boxed ear will never make a full belly ; and I have heard it said that patience is the father of plenty. There's fine ground for a bivouac here, if your Excellency commands. Lord, that I should bring you to bed of a fast !"

He sat scratching his head dolefully while the weary horses began to nibble at the grass and the men to mutter among themselves. Scarce, however, had de Guyon decided that, full or fasting, he could go no further, when the silence was broken of a sudden by the barking of dogs ; a very babel of sound arising up, as it were, from the heart of the obstructing wood. Then lights appeared between the trees, and the voices of men were heard.

"Oh, glory be to God for the path that I have followed!" said Pepin, recovering from his momentary bewilderment. "Yonder, my master, is the Château aux Loups."

"It lies in the thicket, then?"

"Aye, as close surrounded with trees as a fine woman with petticoats. You could no more come up to it without guide than fly to heaven with half a paternoster. Blessed be the holy patron that hath brought me!"

But de Guyon no longer paid heed to him.

"Wind a blast on the horn," said he.

The sleeping forest echoed the music of the note, and the little troop rode on.

CHAPTER III.

GABRIELLE DE VERNET.

PEPIN had spoken the truth about the château. It lay amongst the trees like a kernel in a nut. Many of the gigantic oaks which girdled it about thrust their long branches against the ramparts that looked down upon its narrow fosse. A man might have ridden in the forest for a year, and have known nothing of the turreted, castle-like building whereto Gabrielle de Vernet had, after the death of the Count, withdrawn to keep herself unspotted from the world. Paul de Guyon, halting in parley with a lackey at the wood's edge, could espy neither path nor gateway; and suffered his horse to be led through the mazy labyrinth of tree and bush, until he stood at last before the drawbridge and clattered into the ill-paved courtyard.

"My lady is at her devotions," said the man, "but I doubt not she will see your Excellency at once. Meanwhile, I will look to the comfort of your men."

"Ah," said Pepin, smacking his lips, "an honest soup with lettuce and leeks, a nice piece of bouillé, a frangipani and some green peas *à la bourgeoise.*"

The man looked at him with amazement.

"It is the eve of the feast of St. Philip and St. James," said he simply, "monsieur will not wish to break the fast."

"To break the fast!" gasped Pepin, "aye, my friend, I have the mind to break it and that right soon. But I was ever a man of simple tastes —a well-boiled capon now!"

The servant shrugged his shoulders and turned to de Guyon.

"If only we had known of your

Excellency's coming," said he. "It
was otherwise before my master died.
But now—ah, we are put to shame
in our own house !"

"Suffer no shame on my account,
good friend," said de Guyon, "I am
a soldier and look for a soldier's fare.
Your mistress is at her devotions, did
you say ?"

"In the chapel yonder, monsieur——"

"Then I came fortunately. Pepin, look to the men and behave
yourself. I am going to say my
prayers."

"Ho, ho," said Pepin to himself,
"*mon maître* goes to pray. Surely
the stars will fall !"

The chapel was upon the left side
of the courtyard, a quaint Norman
nook with fine rounded arches and
pilaster-like buttresses, which had
warred with the centuries and won
victories. A stream of light was
poured through its open but richly
carved doorway, and the narrow windows were so many pictures of saints

and angels hung up upon the be-grimed walls. De Guyon, standing in the porch, observed many little shrines with candles burning before them, and he could hear the voice of the priest soft in a rippling monotone of prayer. When at last he ventured to enter, and to kneel at the bottom of the nave, the flicker of tapers and the long shadows they cast in the ashes and upon the bare stone pave-ment, blinded his eyes to any obser-vation of the few worshippers who knelt before the high altar. But the magnificent ornaments of the chapel made themselves plain ; and he doubted no longer those rumours of Gabrielle de Vernet's wealth which had come to the Court and had made "the little Huguenot" a subject for the gossip of the curious and of the king. None but a very rich woman, he said, could have heaped those altars with such jewelled crosses and such inlaid candlesticks. The very cruci-fix nailed to the wall above the pul-pit must have been worth the salary

of an almoner. Soft carpets, unsurpassable carvings of wood, pictures
of the Christ and of saints, shrines
whereon diamonds and rubies and
precious stones caught the tapers'
light, and adding to it their own fires,
scattered dancing rays upon the
gloom, were evidences of an ardent
love of church—and of a well-filled
purse. Whatever might have been
the creed of the girlish mistress of
the Château aux Loups, and there
were many who avowed that in her
heart she despised the Catholic religion, and was even less than a good
Protestant, she yet conformed to
the outward observance of the old
forms. This chapel was an unan-
swerable witness to her generosity.
It remained for the lieutenant to
learn if it were also a witness to her
sincerity.

To de Guyon, steeped in the un-
ending *niaiseries* of the Court, with
the glare of masquerade and banquet
still in his eyes, the chill and gloom
of this chapel were sobering. As he

knelt at the foot of a great pillar and peered into the darkness of the chancel—for the tapers before the tabernacle were unlighted—the reality of his task and the absurdity of it forced themselves upon his mind. It was the king's hope to lure "the little Huguenot" from her forest fastness, and to make sport of her creed ; and —as de Guyon did not doubt—of her honour at the palace. A debauched appetite was made strong again in this thought of so dainty a dish. If only the mistress of the château could be tempted by intrigue to set foot in the palace, the battle was won. St. Anthony himself could not have shut his ears to the apocalypse of license and debauchery of which the king was the arch-priest. What mere intrigue could not accomplish, the wit of madame would ensure. This, at least, was the intention of those who had sent the young lieutenant of the guard to the work. There was scarce a finer man in the palace. His courage and good-nature were notorious.

And he could play a part like Grand-
val himself. Only in the silence of
the chapel did the hazard of the venture occur to him. How would he
fare if "the little Huguenot" read
his purpose? He had but six men
with him. There must have been a
hundred who would rally to the tocsin
of the château. The fanatical warnings of the priest in the forest were
prophetical of the common spirit.
He might be cast into the fosse without, and no men of his company live
to tell the tale of his coming. The
common tongue said that Gabrielle
was a woman of fine spirit. But
that he must learn for himself.

Until this time, he had been un-
able from his place of observation to
see anything of the company in the
chapel. But now, when the priest
had ended the mournful chanting,
little acolytes in scarlet cassocks and
white cottas kindled the tapers upon
the high altar and also those in a
great chandelier beneath the rood-
screen. The new light fell upon a

reredos of marble and gold, almost hidden by vases of white flowers. It fell, too, upon the face of an old priest gorgeously robed in a jewelled cope. While taper-bearers and thurifers prostrated themselves before the Host in the monstrance, and a hidden choir began to sing very sweetly the Latin hymn, "O Salutaris Hostia," de Guyon had eyes for none of these, but only for the little group of worshippers who knelt by the chancel gates. Here were some twelve men and women, all seemingly absorbed in their devotions, all dressed very soberly, and for the most part in plain black. There was not a man amongst them that hid his hair in a wig; not a woman of the company that seemed to know of the coiffure *à boucles badines, au berceau d'amour* or *au mirliton.* Simplicity was the note of it all, and de Guyon, when he had shaken off his surprise, admitted that this simplicity was in pretty harmony with the sombre note of the chapel. He might have been watching so many monks and nuns who had clothed themselves in lay dress—but timidly.

In the centre of the little company, there knelt a girl whose face was hidden from him, but whose figure and pose were infinitely graceful. He was led to believe by the position she occupied that she must be the countess, and that the men at her side were the poets and philosophers who had come to the château to air their graces and to fill their stomachs. For the time being she was occupied entirely with her devotions, and when she raised the smallest of white hands, it was to bury her face in them while she prostrated herself before the upraised Host. Anon, however, the music died away suddenly; the last cloud of incense floated to the vaulted roof; the acolytes extinguished the candles before the altar, and the girl rose and passed down the chapel. De Guyon said to himself that the gossips were right. If a Madonna had come out of one of the pictures

above the shrines, and had stood before him, lending flesh and blood to
the painter's vision, he could scarce
have been more surprised. Such a
delicacy of form and feature he had
hardly seen in all the six years he
had been at Versailles ; had never
known eyes in which so much tenderness and emotion seemed to lie. He
declared that her mouth was like a
rosebud upon which the dew has just
fallen. She held herself with the
grace of a woman grown grey in
practising the courtesies ; yet her
limbs had the roundness and supple-
ness of maturing youth. The black
robe, falling from her shoulders prettily yet without panier, and set off
only with lace at her neck and wrists,
was her best adornment. She wore
no jewels ; not so much as a band
of gold upon her arm. Her brown
hair was simply coiled upon her
head. De Guyon said to himself
that Legros, with all his art, could
not have added to the effect of it.
And with this thought he left the

chapel to await her in the courtyard.

Her greeting was simple, neither
effusive nor lacking welcome.

" I have heard of you, Monsieur
de Guyon, from my Cousin Claude,"
said she, when he had presented his
letters to her ; " you must be tired,
indeed. Let us think of supper before we read even these letters"—and
so turning to the group of men standing behind her, she added simply—

" Gentlemen, let me present you
Monsieur de Guyon, a lieutenant of
his Majesty's Guards. He has ridden far to serve us, and we must
thank him by hastening to supper."

She passed on with a graceful inclination of her head, while servants
conducted de Guyon to a room in the
right wing of the château. Ten minutes later he was supping in the hall.

CHAPTER IV.

THE KINGFISHER AND THE CROWS.

THE lieutenant of the guard was a man to please. His scarlet coat slashed with gold, his fine lace and buckles, his gorgeous sword-belt, showed all the points of his lusty figure in their perfection. There was dormant intellect marked in his eyes, good temper in the well-balanced features of his face, which always wore a self-satisfied smile. Two studies alone occupied him at Versailles or Paris—the study of showy wit and of showy women. Seated by Gabrielle de Vernet's side in the hall of the château he was like a kingfisher among crows. A sense of superiority gave him confidence. He said to himself that it would be easy to shine in such a company.

37

The long table, lighted by heavy
silver candelabra, was arranged in
the form of a horse-shoe. The crows,
broken down wits and poets, display-
ing a ripe eagerness for the repast,
were at the lower end of the hall.
A heavy-browed priest, with hanging
cheeks and a purple cassock, sat upon
the left hand of the hostess. There
was armour in abundance upon the
walls of the panelled apartment ;
and a choir in a gallery at the far end
sang a Latin grace very prettily.
And that done with, the lackeys
busied themselves and the crows began to peck.

Until this moment, de Guyon had
not exchanged two words with the
girl upon his left hand, but the moment that hot soup was placed before
him, he began to rack his brain for
some pleasantry that should please.
He had contrived to turn a pretty
compliment, and was beginning to
blurt it out, when to his great annoy-
ance, she raised her finger, and whispered to him—

" We have yet to read the Gospel of the day."

De Guyon checked the words upon his lips, and turned to his dinner. Notwithstanding the pious hopes of the serving man that Pepin would not break his fast, there was meat set before the young lieutenant ; and the crows, who were busy with dishes of carp and other unsavoury fish, turned greedy eyes upon his plate. Some fine old Burgundy helped him to wash down the repast, but the others, save the priest, drank a thin white wine, and their mouths shrank every time they raised their tumblers. Nor did one of them venture to open his lips, but sat with eyes cast down and unresting jaws, while a young man, who wore a cassock and bands, read the Gospel of the day, and afterwards a sermon by Massillon, of which the note was the ardent denunciation of all profligates.· Then only was the floodgate of talk opened ; then only did the crows begin to caw.

" Well, Monsieur de Guyon, and what news have you to tell me of Paris ?"

The girl at the head of the table turned a pair of searching eyes upon him. Her face wore the suspicion of a smile. He felt that she was looking him through and through. And he returned her glance, putting on the air of a man who could not by any possibility conceal anything.

" Indeed, madame," said he, " I left the Barrière d'Enfer yesterday at daybreak. We count nothing news in Paris that is forty hours old. And it is a week since I have seen Madame de Boufflers."

" Who is better versed in the small talk of the day than any other lady in Paris. What a misfortune for you."

" It is no misfortune which brings me to the Château aux Loups."

She paid no heed to the compliment, resting her chin upon the back of an exceedingly white hand.

" But the people of the château amuse you very much ?" she asked.

"We are never amused by that which we esteem."

She became thoughtful for a minute, continuing to keep her eyes upon him ; but before she spoke again, the purple-robed priest upon her left hand turned from his meat for the first time.

"Present me to monsieur," said he.

"My kinsman, the Abbé Gondy," said she simply.

"Your visit is very welcome to us, monsieur," said the Abbé, bowing ; "though we are not of the world, we are yet weak enough to wish to know what the world does. What says Paris now of the death of Madame Doublet de Persan. Ah, the great folk I have met in her house—St. Palaze — Mairan, Devaur, Perrin ! What a salon it was ! I shall never forget her banquets."

The Abbé looked regretfully at the relics of the fish before him, and helped his memory with a deep sigh, and a second glass of the rich red

Burgundy. But de Guyon, glad to be set going, answered him apace—

"The loss of Madame Doublet de Persan is irretrievable," said he : "we shall not see her like again in Paris. Madame Geoffrin is old ; Madame du Deffand grows tiresome. You have heard, monsieur, that her Majesty of Russia is anxious to carry the fashion of the city to the *bourgeoisie* of St. Petersburg. Madame Geoffrin has refused her twice. Madame du Deffand declines to be the instrument. Society, she says, is made up of persons incapable of knowledge, thought, and feeling. They have enough of those in Muscovy already."

"Ah !" cried the Abbé, with an unecclesiastical laugh, "and that is true. If all one hears of her Majesty is well said, she has as many affairs as a grisette of Bordeaux. But I never listen to such tales myself. Charity, monsieur, is a great virtue. Let us cultivate it always."

He smacked his lips over the wine, and Gabrielle de Vernet spoke again.

"You are riding to the palace at Fontainebleau, monsieur?" she asked de Guyon.

He was ready with his answer.

"I am riding to the palace when it is madame's pleasure to ride with me."

"My pleasure? Oh, my dear Monsieur de Guyon, what should I do at Fontainebleau?"

"Then you have not read of his Majesty's invitation, madame?"

"Certainly, I have not. I do not love letters."

He looked at her incredulously.

"But a command from the king; that is different."

"Not at all—it is the same thing; an expression of wishes one does not feel for a person in whom one has no interest. His Majesty's letter may wait the morning. I am in no hurry, and I am sure that he is not."

"And the note from your Cousin Claude?"

"Oh, my Cousin Claude writes always of himself—the subject in which he is most concerned."

De Guyon bit his lip. The woman was either a delightful actress, or a pretty simpleton gone crazy in the practice of a discredited creed.

"We have need of example at the Court, madame," said he. "You have heard the saying of the Abbé Cozer : 'In order to be something, a great part of the nobility is plunged into nothingness.'"

"And you think that I should be an example ?"

"His Majesty is sure of it."

"But—you yourself ?"

"I am of the king's opinion, as a soldier should ever be."

To his surprise she now laughed lightly.

"Should I have you for a pupil ?" she asked.

"One of the most faithful."

"And you would walk with me in the park if I wore no other gown than this ?"

"I would look for no greater honour. The best ornament of beauty is simplicity, madame."

_____

"As the best weapon of intrigue is truth, monsieur."

Her mood passed for a moment to severity. Her lips were pursed up, her eyes searched him curiously. It was only for a moment, however. Presently she began to laugh again, and she murmured, as if to herself, some doggerel in which a wag had caricatured the fashionable coiffure of the hour—

> "*Soutiens, Jasmin, je succombe,*
> *Et prends bien garde, faquin*
> *Qui si ma coiffure tombe*
> *Tu auras ton compte demain.*"

"They tell me," said she, "that women now wear their hair a foot high."

"To conceal the smallness of their heads, believe me, madame."

"What an excellent reason."

"Which, in your case, I venture to think would be no reason at all."

"A hit, a hit!" chimed in the Abbé, who had been busy with the wine-bottle. "They do say that the women at the Court nowadays carry much virtue on their skulls and little in their breasts. But, for myself, I pay no heed to these scandals. The tongue of the world is very wicked, Monsieur de Guyon."

"It is often very amusing," said de Guyon.

"And the more amusing because the less true," said madame.

"Exactly ; truth is a very ordinary faculty to cultivate."

"And, therefore, you let it lie fallow."

De Guyon bit his lip again. In all their talk it seemed to him that the slim and graceful girl in the black robe was laughing at him. Accustomed to mould women to his mood, to bend them'before the graces which it was the business of his life to cultivate, he knew not how to meet an antagonist against whom flattery was no weapon, and wit no defence. Nor was he willing to admit that he had cut a poor figure.

"I am tired to-night," he said, " but to-morrow——"

The supper being now done, the
countess rose from the table and led
the way into a little boudoir, not in-
elegantly furnished, and betraying
nothing of that ascetic rigour else-
where to be observed.

" We will talk of all these things
in the morning, when you ride with
me, monsieur," said she. " To-night
we must amuse you."

He could not find it on his tongue
to tell her that already she amused
him—nay, fascinated him beyond any
woman he had known. The vigour
and freshness of her mind were already conquering him. He felt like
a boy that had been beaten when he
sat at her side to listen to the harpist,
and to the ballads of one of the crows,
delivered with a nasal drawl and a
precision which were ludicrous. And
when at last she bade him good-
night, and he went up to the great
oak-panelled bedchamber, he carried
with him the memory of a sweet girlish face, of a woman's eyes that
seemed to read his whole soul, of a

voice which was soft and pleasing as the clear note of a bell.

From the window of his bedchamber he could look out upon a great sweep of the forest, flooded with the moonbeams. The scene—rich in soft lights, in tremulous whisperings and suggestions of sleep—fell in with his mood. From the inner court of the château he could hear snatches of song floating upon the stillness of the night; the harsh voice of the rogue Pepin, the deep, baying laugh of the musketeers, spoke of the passing of the wine-cup and of the camp jest. But the woodlands slept, and the rare cries of beasts or notes of birds were like challenges of sentinels that guarded the moon-lit ramparts.

The spell of it all was irresistible, dream-bearing. Long de Guyon sat at his open window, busy with his thoughts. And this thought was above all others: that the mistress of the château must not go to the palace, though her absence cost him his command.

CHAPTER V.

THE Abbé Gondy descended from the grassy hill upon which he had watched de Guyon and Gabrielle de Vernet set out to the hunt ; and so soon as the last of the horsemen had disappeared into the thick wood which lay upon the borders of the home park, he returned with slow steps to the château. For the first time for some years the Abbé was thinking. His ponderous mind creaked on its hinges : he had a problem to solve, and he admitted that he could make nothing of it.

At the door of the stables he found the rogue Pepin, basking in the glorious sunshine.

" Good morning, my friend," said the Abbé, suddenly conceiving a notion; "so you have deserted your master?"

"Aye, and that's God's truth, father—for who would shake his body on a horse when he can lie back down in the blessed sunlight? Blood of Paul! I have no stomach for boar's meat when I must do the catching."

"You are a philosopher, my son."

"If so be that your philosopher waits while other men work, I am that same person."

The Abbé smiled.

"I like your teaching, friend," said he.

"Oh, I am a faithful pupil of Holy Church, my father."

"Would that we had more of them in these evil times," said the Abbé, raising his eyes solemnly to heaven, but instantly casting them down again.

"You have breakfasted, my son?" he asked, a moment later.

"In the matter of a snack I have done fairly well, monsieur; but should you be led to inquire if my girths are drawn tight, so to speak, I would even answer you, nay !"

The Abbé's eyes twinkled.

"Yesterday was a fast," said he : "to-day is a feast. You shall drink a cup of wine at my own board."

Pepin was on his legs in a moment. Five minutes later the same legs were dangling beneath the Abbé's groaning table.

"God send a saint every day of the year !" said Pepin, filling his mouth with slices from the breast of a well-boiled capon.

"Amen to that !" cried the Abbé, drinking a glass of luscious red wine.

"And a fat capon for sinners to fast upon."

"Let me fill your glass," said the Abbé, with oily condescension.

"You are too good, my father."

"I am the servant of the servants of God," murmured the Abbé, while his hand which held the decanter shook beyond concealment. "You have been with Monsieur de Guyon long, my friend ?"

"I was with his father at Minden, monsieur. *Dieu!* I had three at once upon my sword!"

Pepin lied very discreetly. The truth was that de Guyon had picked him up the previous day at the Barrière d'Enfer, but the memory of Minden allowed him to pose as an old family retainer. The Abbé, however, knew nothing of this, and, assuming that he was talking to a confidential servant, he opened his heart freely.

"You are accompanying your master to the palace?"

Pepin had not the faintest notion whither de Guyon was carrying him, so he said, and there were tears in his eyes.

"I follow him to the world's end, *mon père.*"

"You know why he has come here?"

Pepin did not know, but he was far too wise to betray his ignorance. With his tongue in his cheek, he made a grimace at the Abbé.

" Ah," said the priest, with a sly laugh, " you are a cunning fellow."

" I am as God made me, holy father."

" I always said," continued the Abbé, as if to himself, " that madame would hear of us."

" It's known in all Paris," said Pepin, clutching at a straw.

The Abbé appeared not to notice the remark.

" Your master has many friends at Court ?" he asked suddenly.

" Their names would fill a book," said Pepin.

" And he has come straight to us from the king ?"

" From the king !" cried Pepin, observing on a sudden the opportunity to appear knowing; " ha, ha, that's a fine story.   From the king ! What an idea !"

The Abbé looked at him searchingly.

" Fill your glass," said he.

Pepin did so.

" If you will tell me the name of

the person whose messenger your master is, I will give you ten gold pieces," said the Abbé.

" Ten gold pieces," murmured Pepin, making another grimace ; " oh, but I am a faithful servant, monsieur."

" Then twenty pieces," urged the Abbé.

He counted the money out upon the table—but covered it with his hand.

" One moment, my friend," said he ; " when did your master last have audience of his Majesty ?"

" Audience of his Majesty ! Ha, ha, you joke, Monsieur l'Abbé !"

The priest began to put the money into the bag again.

" We do not understand each other yet," said he.

" Nay," said Pepin, " we understand each other perfectly. My master last had audience of his Majesty nine months ago, when he was sub-lieutenant at the Louvre."

" You lie," said the Abbé coolly,

replacing all the money in the bag;
" nine months ago your master was
in Corsica. And he spoke with the
king at Versailles five days ago."

" Ah ! what tricks my memory
plays with me," said Pepin, taken
unawares ; " but about those ten
pieces, monsieur ?"

" You see how well they go in this
bag," remarked the Abbé, at the
same time withdrawing the decanter
from the other's reach ; " we will
talk of them again, my son, when
your memory is in no mood for tricks.
Meanwhile, I have to say my office."

Pepin scratched his head. He saw
that he had made a mess of things.

" *Parbleu !* that was a good breakfast," cried he—but the Abbé already
had his breviary in his hand.

" *Bon jour*, monsieur !" said Pepin,
lurching out.

" Impostor !" murmured the Abbé,
kneeling at his faldstool.

" What Burgundy !" exclaimed
Pepin, staggering to the stables to
sleep.

The Abbé's devotions were interspersed with strange thoughts that morning. His eyes would wander from the pages of his breviary ; his busy brain employed itself with anything but worship. The coming of de Guyon had upset him strangely. It had even suggested to him the possibility that Gabrielle de Vernet might marry again. And how would he fare with a master at the château ? He said to himself that he might fare badly ; might in an extreme case be driven out to some mean care of souls in some mean hamlet. "Far better," whispered the devil in his ear, "that she should go to Versailles, and leave you in possession of the Château aux Loups. She may become as the others, but you, at any rate, have tried to keep her to the faith. And she is a pure woman."

"*Vade retro Satanas*," murmured the Abbé piously ; and then he fell to reading the words :—"Brethren, be sober and watch."

CHAPTER VI.

IN THE BOWER OF VIOLETS.

GABRIELLE DE VERNET was a perfect horsewoman. De Guyon said to himself twenty times as he rode with her on the morning after his coming to the château that she would surely break her neck. Somehow, he found that he was more anxious for her safety than for his own. She looked so girlish with her golden-brown hair coiled loosely on her neck, and her tiny hands controlling a great horse that might have carried a commander. And no difficulty of the road was too great for her nerve or her daring. He shuddered again and again when she rode blindly through the labyrinthine way of copse thicket, or galloped wildly where the sward was soft and the way was open.

There were moments when he said
that she must certainly be killed.
And he himself was no mountebank
in the saddle.

Even to a man accustomed to the
gaudy pictures of life at Court, the
scene was no unworthy one. The
green coats and feathered hats of the
woodlanders, the changing beauties
of the forest; the baying of the
hounds, the winding blast of horns,
the thud of hoofs upon the rich green
turf braced his mind to exhilaration in the sport. And when to this
there was added that fascination
which the company of Gabrielle de
Vernet already cast upon him, his
heart went out to the spirit of the
morning, and all the burning fevers
of intrigue and ambition and debauchery seemed to leave him.

At the first she had ridden with the
others, with a fearlessness which
many a man might have envied. But
when they had galloped some miles
almost upon the outskirts of the forest, it appeared to de Guyon that she

was drawing away from the chase,
and seeking to plunge into the
darker places of the woods. The
note of the horns died down in the
distance ; the voice of the hounds
were faint echoes in the hollows ;
and still she rode on through groves
of close set pines and tangles of
bramble ; over swards carpeted with
violets and meadows of soft sand ; by
dark pools and bubbling brooks.
When at last she drew rein it was at
a thicket's edge in a grass glade odor-
ous with the perfume of sweet flowers ; there one of her own serving
men came out to greet her.

" Our ride is over, Monsieur de
Guyon," said she, jumping lightly
from her horse, " and here we should
find our breakfast. Did you think
that I was going to lose you in the
forest ?"

She was blushing deeply ; but it
was with the blush of a young girl's
health. It seemed to de Guyon that
she had left at the château that
stately dignity of speech and bearing

which he had remarked at their first meeting. Nor did he know in which mood he found her the more charming. While he had thought overnight that there was no woman at Versailles to be compared to her as the graceful mistress of a household, he now said that this girlish freedom was unsurpassable in its charm and attractiveness. And her riding-dress showed her pretty figure to exceeding advantage ; the quaint round hat in which she had gone to the hunt gave piquancy to the freshness of her young face. He said to himself that the wonder was, not that the king now desired to see her, but that she had not been lured to the palace long ago. Yet he trembled at the thought of her being there ; found himself in some way posing mentally as her protector from ills which it seemed a crime to think upon.

The nook in which they were to breakfast was the one she called her bower. In part it was of nature's making ; in part the work of her own

gardeners, who had trained honey-
suckle about the little wooden pavilion and had almost smothered it in
roses. Here, in the depths of the
glen, a clear pool of water caught the
sun's rays streaming through a canopy of boughs and branches, and
showed gold and silver fish basking
in the warmth, or feeding on the ripe
green weeds which flourished on the
pebbly bed. A little balcony, pleas-
antly shaded by a roof of flowering
creeper, was built over the pond, and
the breakfast to which de Guyon had
been invited was spread out upon a
little wooden table on this balcony.
He saw at once that only two chairs
were set ; and for a moment he had
hopes of this discovery. Was it possible that Gabrielle de Vernet was
going to make love to him ?

This pleasing speculation was soon
at rest. Directly the girl began to
speak to him he knew that no such
thoughts were in her mind. The
pretty speech he had framed died
away upon his lips. He began men-

tally to pay her a new homage. She
was so different from any woman he
had known. He felt like a child before a mistress—and yet he was drawn
towards her as towards one whom all
the world must love. He said that
it would be heaven itself to hold her
in his arms ; then remembered that
he had come to her that he might
carry her to the shame of the Court.
It was a pitiful errand, indeed ; it
seemed the more pitiful when she began to speak of it fearlessly.

"You are wondering why I left
the hunt and brought you to my
bower ?" she asked while she heaped
her plate with fresh fruit, and the
servant filled their glasses with a
pleasing yellow wine.

"*Parbleu!* since your bower is so
pleasant a place, why should I ask
any such question ?"

"It would be very natural if you
had done so," said she, unmindful of
the compliment, "and I don't know
that I am not treating you very ill.
But I promised myself that I would

talk of your message this morning—
and my curiosity is your punishment.
I have now read my cousin Claude's
letter, in which he conveys to me the
king's earnest wish that I should
present myself at Versailles. You, I
understand, are sent to emphasise
that wish."

It was a very direct question, and
he saw no way by which he might
evade it.

" Certainly, that is so," he stammered at last. " His Majesty's wish
is to be read as a command in a matter like this. I will tell you frankly
that I am sent to escort you to the
palace, where the king would be glad
to consult you upon many subjects
connected with—with——"

" With what, Monsieur de Guyon ?
Really you provoke my curiosity
again."

He felt that she was laughing at
him, and in his embarrassment his
tongue failed him.

" Oh,'' she said, continuing in a
spirit of raillery, " you are a very bad

ambassador, Monsieur de Guyon. I
shall really have to help you myself."

" I am afraid that you speak truth.
I am a soldier, madame, and my
principal occupation is to obey."

" Even when obedience concerns a
woman's honour?"

He had no answer to give to her—
his mind was bent like a whip in her
hands.

" Yes, my friend," she continued,
sparing him in nothing, " I can scarce
think that you have lived under the
king's roof for five years without
knowing well what his Majesty's gra-
cious wish implies. You ask me if I
will go to the palace? I answer you
by another question—does the dove
go willingly to the cage, the deer to
the stable? Does the man who has
breathed God's air upon the hills
sleep at his ease in a cellar? Here,
with the children who love me, with
the forest for my home, with the
worship of God in Jesus Christ for
my occupation, I find life rich in
treasure, as she is always rich to those

that deal well with her. Think you that I would surrender these my pleasures at the nod of any king— even at the nod of the well-beloved? Oh, Monsieur de Guyon, you know that I would not."

She had spoken quickly, the effort suffusing her face with a glow of pink; her eyes bright with earnestness of purpose. De Guyon, accustomed to the restraint of the women of the Court, to the practice of verbal insincerities, listened to her with amazement. Here was a woman who believed in Christ—yet a woman with warm blood in her veins; no recluse of the cell, but a living, breathing entity, to listen to whom was to hear a voice as from another world. Her very frankness gave him courage; all the fine phrases with which he had hoped to ensnare had long passed from his mind. He answered her in plain words as she wished.

"Madame," said he, "it is ill to put upon the servant the designs of

the master. I am the servant of
King Louis. If he says go, I go ; or
stay, and I stay. How then would
you make me your adviser ? Indeed,
this visit is none of my planning. I
knew not of it until the hour in which
I was bidden to set out. It is only
when you speak to me like this that I
am able to answer frankly. As a
soldier, I say to you, come with me
to the palace ; as a friend, I urge
you to remain at your château as long
as the king will permit."

" As long as the king will permit !
Then he adds threats to the expression of his pleasure ?"

" His Majesty does not love to be
contradicted, 'madame."

" Nay, but you shall contradict
him for me ; you shall return this
very night with my message. If I
am to go to Versailles——"

" To Fontainebleau. His Majesty
will be there on Sunday next to receive you."

" Oh, his Majesty is very thoughtful. See, my dear Monsieur de

Guyon, how he would shield me from prying eyes."

"He judged that the journey would be less fatiguing ; you are but five leagues from the palace of Francis, are you not ?"

" Six exactly, *mon ami*—yet far enough to prove a heavy burden when his Majesty comes to carry me."

" To carry you !"

" I will go no other way. He shall take me in his own arms. Think you, Monsieur de Guyon, that you could carry me six leagues ? Certainly you could not."

De Guyon thought that he would be happy if the attempt were permitted to him ; but he said nothing of this, harking back rather to the message he must bear.

" The king comes to the château on Saturday about sundown," said he ; " I am to meet him there with news of you."

" Then that you have. You will tell him that Gabrielle de Vernet will come to the Court when he shall be pleased to carry her there."

He stared at her now with blank astonishment.

"It would cost me my command," he stammered.

She looked at him with a little contempt.

"Your command, Monsieur de Guyon—would you buy that at such a price ?"

"*Ma foi!*" said he ; but—you do not know ; I am poor and without friends ; the king trusts me in this——"

She laughed loudly.

"Well," said she, "you are but a simpleton after all. Come, you have eaten no breakfast. And since you must remain with me some days, I must see that you preserve your appetite. We will talk of this again. Let us think of going homeward now."

For a moment he sat looking into her laughing eyes. He seemed about to answer her, but minutes passed before the words came to his lips. At last he said quite suddenly—

"Madame de Vernet, there is no need to talk of this again. I will take your message."

"And resign hopes of a command?"

"If it must be."

"But you have said that it must be."

"Very well then, I will resign hopes of a command."

"You are a brave man, Monsieur de Guyon."

"But I have my reward," said he.

The look which he gave her betrayed all his admiration and growing love. For the first time she was embarrassed in his presence, and made haste to be put upon her horse. Nor did she speak again while they rode through glade and meadow to the château, turning her head away from him, and answering him with monosyllables. She had begun to believe that de Guyon was a man after all. And in this, her womanhood was conquering her.

CHAPTER VII.

THE ABBÉ GONDY WRITES A SERMON.

THE Abbé Gondy sat in his study on the morning of the Friday following the coming of de Guyon. His swollen feet were wrapped in woollen slippers ; the violet girdle round his waist was loosened—for the morning was hot, and thunder hung over the forest. Before him on the great carved oak table there were rough notes of a sermon he was to preach at the Mass on Sunday ; by his side, a basin of Mocha coffee was steaming.

"Brethren, love one another," wrote the Abbé, and then he put his pen down. "She is not going to the palace," he thought, "because de Guyon has bungled it. The man is little better than a fool. I believe

he is in love with her himself.
Mother of God, if she were to marry
again I should have no room here.
That smooth-faced soldier would
take a pipe in his hand and go playing to the sheep. But if she were at
the palace and like the others, she
would hardly return."

"Even as I have loved you," wrote
the Abbé, but again his thoughts
wandered. "This life is very pleasant," he said to himself, "and I find
myself well in this air. There is
abundance for all, while in villages
and hamlets not ten leagues from
here, holy priests are starving. A
new master might come here with
other views. He might even deny
the faith ; be unprepared to tread
that narrow way to which I am leading my children. In any case, I
should have to give up these apartments. But if she went to the palace
it might even be that I should remain
master to my death. There is virtue
in an ' if,' " thought the Abbé.

The reflection deepened the gloom

of his depression. Since the death
of the Comte de Vernet, who had
been stricken down by small-pox five
weeks after his marriage to Gabrielle,
the Abbé had lived in close commu-
nication with the young mistress of
the château; had come to know her
well as a creature of noble if quick
impulses, of a belief in God at any
rate, of a strong will and of a warm
heart. Married while a mere child
to the count, life had not scattered
the bloom of her girlhood, nor awak-
ened in her those instincts which
might have been at once her safe-
guard and her peril. A wife but not
a mother, she had something of the
innocence of the maid and of the
mind of the woman. The Abbé said
to himself that no temptation could
be found sufficiently strong to taint
this innocence or break this will.
He was only an utterly selfish man.
The fall of Gabrielle de Vernet would
have been a deep sorrow to him. It
was just because he knew that she
was of mind enough to cope with

danger successfully that he wished her at the palace. When a voice whispered to him that the peril to her honour was terrible, he said that the devil spoke. He called to mind the words of the apostle, that no soul should be tempted beyond that which it could bear. And at this, he drank his coffee with relish.

"Brethren, to-day I would set before you some consideration of this holy counsel, that we love one another," wrote the Abbé quickly, and with some fine flourishes of his goose quill. He was well started now, and he did not put his pen down until he had filled four pages with closely-written notes. Nevertheless was the thought of de Guyon hovering about his mind, and of a sudden it presented itself in an aspect so alarming that he sat back in his chair, and let the wind scatter the treasured pages upon the soft carpet at his feet.

"*Dieu!*" said he, " this man leaves us to-morrow—but what message is he taking to the king? What excuse

will he make for her? Will he urge
that my counsels prevented her?
Saints and angels! that would send
me to the Bastille. And he would
be rewarded and return to marry her.
She is in love with his pretty face, if
I know anything of women. The
way she speaks of him, too—a good
man to be snatched from wickedness
and made honest by example. Bah!
a fop and a farceur to be reckoned
with. I must think of this. I have
an account to settle."

The Abbé thought of it, long and
earnestly. So absorbing was the
problem that twelve o'clock struck
and he forgot to say the Angelus.
Far from it—for he was then unlock-
ing a drawer in his bureau, and occu-
pying himself with an exquisite mini-
ature which he laid upon his table and
gazed at with affection. The man
was a fine judge of art, and the paint-
ing staring at him from the dainty
gold frame was art in her highest
perfection. It was the portrait of
Gabrielle de Vernet, painted on ivory

---

by Richard Cosway, when that master was the guest of Claude Vernet in Paris. The countess had given it to the Abbé as an Easter gift just a year ago, and it was with a bitter struggle that he had made up his mind to part with it. Only, in fact, when he had convinced himself that some bold step must be taken to save his own skin, did he return it to its case, and strike the gong at his side.

" Dominique."

" Monsieur."

" Is the guide Pepin in the courtyard ?"

" He is sleeping in the pavilion by the lake, monsieur."

" Tell him I wish to see him."

The man left, and the Abbé turned again to his desk, taking from it that identical bag which he had held under Pepin's nose three days before. When the guide entered the room, the first thing that he saw were the ten gold pieces he had lusted for spread out on the table.

"*Bon jour*, Monsieur l'Abbé," said Pepin gaily.

"*Bon jour*, Monsieur Pepin."

"You sent for me?"

"Sit down, my son. I wish to talk to you, since you leave us to-morrow."

"To-morrow!" cried Pepin, casting his eyes about to see where the Burgundy might be.

"Your master has not told you, then?"

"The devil he hasn't."

"You know that madame does not accompany you?"

"That's common gossip, my father."

"Exactly. But what say the men?"

"Oh, they say anything. They wag their tongues like cows' tails. A shabby lot, on my word."

"Yes; but when they wag their tongues what do you hear?"

"Anything — everything. Some say that when next they come back they will leave yonder lieutenant where light is dear and air costs money—in a cell, *mon père.*"

The Abbé reflected for a moment.

" Would you like a glass of wine, Monsieur Pepin ?"

" Aye—what wine it was !" murmured Pepin, rolling his eyes and his tongue.

The Abbé struck his gong again. When the guide had gulped down a great cup of the Burgundy, the priest drew his chair nearer to him.

" My son," said he, " I find you to be a man of large discernment."

" Aye, there you have it, my father," cried Pepin ; " a man of large discernment. Body of John ! there's not a man of a larger between here and the Invalides." At the same time he said to himself, " What does the old rogue want now ?"

" And a man to be trusted," urged the Abbé.

" If there's one that doubts it, monsieur, I shall know how to defend my honour."

The Abbé smiled, remembering

that Pepin's weapon was a four-holed flageolet.

"Undoubtedly, Monsieur Pepin," said he ; "you are a man of courage. See how I make you my confidant, even going so far"—and here the Abbé bent over until his mouth was almost at Pepin's ear—"even going so far as to ask you what part people think I have played in bringing about madame's refusal to go to the palace."

Pepin scratched his head. "The Abbé is measuring his own neck," said he ; "it will pay me to frighten him." And then he gave his answer.

"*Corbleu!* Monsieur l'Abbé, what's the good of hiding things. All the world knows why the king is refused. Your holy words—Mother of God ! they moved even me."

The Abbé winced, and raised his hand in a gesture of dissent.

"No, no, Monsieur Pepin ; it does not concern me at all. Heaven forbid that such a suspicion should come upon a humble servant of his Majesty."

"Eh?" exclaimed Pepin; "but surely you would not have her go?"

"I? My son, I would not harm a hair of her head. But the king's command—think of that!"

Pepin thought of it. His reply was not a pretty one: sticking his tongue in his cheek, he made a grimace at the priest, and then pointed to the coins on the table.

"What of those gold pieces, my father?" he asked suddenly.

"They are for you, my friend."

Pepin stretched out his hand. The Abbé covered the money with his palms.

"If," he continued, "you are able to do a service for me."

Pepin drew back his hand.

"By the Mass," said he, "you know how to plague a man."

"Indeed, my son, that would be an ill thing to do. But the labourer must prove worthy of his hire; and, first, I would know if you ride with de Guyon to-morrow?"

"*Dieu!* he would fare ill without me !"

" And at the palace you are to find the king, alone, eh ?"

Pepin made another grimace. The Abbé drew his chair still nearer.

" And his Majesty being alone, or with very few attendants, it might be possible to slip a packet and a letter into his hand."

" As easy as a paternoster."

" For which service you are to have ten pieces now, and ten more when you shall prove to me that it has been accomplished."

Pepin nodded his head in rhythm with the Abbé's words.

" Ten more when it shall have been accomplished. Holy saints, Monsieur l'Abbé, what a friend you are buying."

" You will carry the packet carefully : it is of great worth. And the letter !"

" I will carry them like the sacrament."

The Abbé turned to his desk, and

wrote precisely seven words upon a large sheet of paper. They were these: "Let the king beware of his ambassador." Then he folded the paper and sealed it.

"Monsieur Pepin," said he, "there is no name to this document; but should you be asked by his Majesty whence it comes, you know how to answer?"

"Aye, that I do," said Pepin. "It was given to me by a stranger on the wayside."

"Fool!" said the Abbé testily. "It was given to you by *me*. But that is for the king's ear alone."

Pepin put the packet in the breast of his jerkin, the money in his pouch.

"The devil of an Abbé!" said he, when he was out in the courtyard.

But the Abbé was at his prayers.

CHAPTER VIII.

MASKING IN THE WOODS.

WHILE the venerable Abbé was writing his sermon upon love, de Guyon was walking in the park of the château waiting for the coming of Gabrielle de Vernet. It was a feast day, and a procession of white-robed children, bearing flowers and banners and lighted candles, had just passed by the glistening lake, and so had entered a wood in the heart of which the chapel of the Virgin had been built. De Guyon listened to the notes of their hymn, dying away in the groves and thickets, and then walked slowly to the open lawns before the southern gate of the house—for tables were set here, and the villagers from many a mile round were coming in to share the hospitality of the woman they adored, and to hold carnival in her park. It was good to see the honest faces of the woodlanders in their liveries of green; the red cheeks and dark eyes of the country girls, all ready for any play they might hap upon; eager to anticipate, perhaps, that moment when the evening would come and some of those great fellows about them would have burdens in their arms. And it was no less good to behold the well-covered tables, the great casks of sound wine, the piles of fruit, the sweetmeats, the fantastic cakes, the fat capons.

Everywhere, indeed, the usually silent forest echoed the music of the horns, the lighter note of laughter, the merry voices of the girls, the neighing of horses. Here and there, beneath some great elm or oak, you might come upon a wandering musician drawn to the château by rumour of the feast, and now scraping his fiddle or blowing his flute for the delectation of the country wenches, all eager for the merry dance. Horsemen rode in from many an outlying station ; priests were to be seen among the people, and were welcomed by them. And when the angry clouds, which at one time had promised thunder, rolled away to the east, and the sun shone upon the sparkling lakes, and the breeze blew fresh and sweet, it was a morning to call even the dreamer to life.

De Guyon, standing beneath the shade of a great oak tree, looked upon the scene and found it powerless to lift the gloom off his mind. He could not but contrast the simplicity, the freshness, the innocence of it with the extravagance, the weariness and the guilt of those feverish masks he was so well accustomed to at Versailles. The light laughter of these country girls, the manly speech of the men, the naïveté of their pleasures would have been a jest to him a week ago. But that was before he knew Gabrielle de Vernet.

" *Dieu !*" said he, " she will make

a monk of me;" and he laughed
aloud at the thought. Yet there was
something very sweet in the contem-
plation of that seclusion which would
keep him always at her side. For
some days now, he, the wit and fine
gentleman, had lived like a priest,
and fared little better than a *reli-
gieux;* had gone to Mass at dawn, had
been content to sit out vespers and
compline, had thought nothing of
clothes for his back or epigram for
his tongue. The silence, the sweet-
ness, the exhilaration of the forest
had entered into his life ; awakening
his mind to the knowledge of a content he had not hitherto known. He
was lifted up out of himself ; carried
to that high place of the spirit wherefrom man may look down upon the
warfare of the passions, may hear the
crying of those in darkness. And he
said to himself that surely it was a
vision come to cheat him, since the
morrow must bring the mists again.

Of the morrow, for a truth, he
could have little hope. He was to

leave at dawn for the château of
Francis and of Henry Quatre, bearing a message which could bring him
no favour nor hope of reward. He
had set out to Fontainebleau, happy
in that he had come to play the humble part of a trusted intriguer ; he
would return to those that sent him,
pleading his own failure, despising
the intrigue. What the aftermath
might be he did not care, if only he
might return to the forest to the feet
of the little Huguenot who had
opened his eyes to such visions.

The crying of many voices in the
park, a new and louder note of music, the galloping of horses called
him from dreamland to the scene before him. Gabrielle de Vernet had
now come down from the chapel, and
surrounded by a lusty body of green-
coated foresters, she made her way
to the high table. He said that it
was good thus to see her worshipped
by those to whom she had given her
life ; good to see her as a thing of
flesh and blood and warm human

sympathies, enlarged and not confined by the discipline to which she submitted. At no time could it have been urged that the ascetic side of her nature overweighed the womanly instinct. She was born for love and marriage—not for the recluse's cell.

De Guyon took his seat at the high table; the Abbé waddled out of the château and raised three fingers in benediction of the multitude; the musicians scraped as they had not scraped before; the feast opened with a flourish of trumpets and a lively babble of tongues. The girl who presided over it had a word and a look for everyone; the lieutenant had a word and a look only for her; the Abbé only for his plate. When the eating and drinking at length were done with (and the foresters had appetites which were to be measured only by hours), the masqueraders began their play in the park, some making believe to be fauns, some sylphs, some spirits of the woods. Warmed with the invigorating wine,

the village girls set themselves with
trembling heels to the dance ; the
fiddlers thrashed their fiddles in melo-
dious ecstasies ; the jesters raised
their shrill voices ; the woodmen
puckered up their lips in hope of
kisses ; the lovers broke away to the
woods to whisper vows in shady
glens. It was passing late in the
afternoon when at last de Guyon
found himself alone with Gabrielle,
and able to speak of the shadow
which the morrow would cast upon
his life, and, as he hoped, upon hers.
They had walked slowly from the
park and come into a little glen, in
the heart of which a brook was bubbling. There was the shadow of as-
pens here, the perfume of violets and
of wild roses ; the fitful song of the
reed-warbler and the wagtail. A
grassy bank, grown over with prim-
roses, served them well for seat ; and
here they rested, while from the distant park the hum of voices and the
light music of the dance came to
them on the waves of the wind. But

the spirit of the glen was one of silence ; and minutes passed before
either of them spoke.

"Well, Monsieur de Guyon," said
she at last, "I don't find you very
witty to-day."

"Indeed," said he, seeking to look
straight into her eyes, "but I have
waited long for the opportunity."

She did not answer him at once,
but began to twist a posy of the prim-
roses. A glow of crimson suffused
her face. There was so much tenderness in his voice that she no longer
looked into his eyes—and she had
ceased to smile.

"You must know," said she, breaking the embarrassing silence with an
effort, "that this is one of the great
days of my year——"

"Henceforth it will be the greatest
day of mine," said he, feeling that
whatever might come of it, he would
not leave her with the word un-
spoken.

"To amuse is as much the duty of
those who rule as to educate," she

went on, making no reference to his compliment. " Three times every year my people keep holiday in the park. I encourage them to feel that they have some interest in the maintenance of my home—that they have a friend here. Friendship, after all, is a creed, Monsieur de Guyon."

De Guyon had thought so little of any religion at all, that he was quite out of his depth when he tried to reply to her.

" This life," said he, " this to-day which is as yesterday, this to-morrow which must be as to-day, does it never weary you, never pall, never set you longing for that other life beyond your gates?"

She smiled at him now.

" When my life shall make me love less, then will I think of yours."

" Of mine?"

" Surely, since you throw down the glove for it. But tell me, *mon ami*, what do they say of the Château aux Loups at the palace? Indeed, I am very curious to know."

De Guyon sat thinking while a minute passed.

"They call you 'the little Huguenot,' believing you to be in heart a Protestant, as your husband was," said he at length, and quite bluntly. "They told me that you lived on herbs and slept in a cell."

"And that was all?"

"Certainly it was not; they said also that you were—well——"

"Well, what, Monsieur de Guyon? How you love to pique my curiosity."

He hesitated to use the word; but remembering that she was, above all else, a woman, he made bold at last to venture it.

"*Parbleu!*" said he. "I will not keep it from you. They spoke of your beauty."

She looked up at him quickly.

"It was unkind of them to deceive you."

"To deceive me? Oh, madame!"

She was now almost lying upon the grass, her head propped upon her elbows, her piquant oval face

resting upon her hands. She had
dressed herself in white for the mask,
and the ribbons at her neck and upon
her breast gave her the air of a little
school-girl just come out of a con-
vent. It seemed odd to de Guyon
to call her " Madame," and when he
had uttered the words, he could not
help himself but must look into her
great laughing eyes and fall in with
her merry humour.

" *Ciel!*" said he, lying so close to
her that their faces almost touched.
" I begin to feel like a father to you—
madame."

" And to act like a cousin," she exclaimed, but without drawing away
from him. " Indeed, I shall think
that you wish to confess me."

" I could find no happier vocation ;
but it is I that should confess."

" I am all ears. What do you confess, monsieur ?"

" The will that once would have
done you an injury."

" Of which guilt—— ?"

" I am duly penitent."

"And for penance?"

"I leave you at dawn."

She became serious in a moment, casting down her eyes and playing nervously with the flowers she had picked. But he, longing for her with an ardent passion—the first guiltless passion of his life—pursued his questioning.

"You give me absolution?" he asked in a low voice.

"I give you my friendship," she replied, looking up, and with tenderness, into his eyes.

"Your friendship!" he exclaimed. "Oh, I will treasure that! Would to God it were something more!"

The fervour of his words seemed to trouble her.

"Friendship," she said, speaking very earnestly, "is a woman's best gift. She has nothing else."

"But her love?"

"That she cannot give or hold. The power is not hers. And friendship, Monsieur de Guyon, is the gateway of love."

"If it should be so for me, Gabrielle?"

"Dear friend," she answered, while he could hear his own heart beating, "what will be is known to God alone. Let us lift up our hearts to Him."

He took her hand and held it between both of his.

"I am not worthy to touch your lips, Gabrielle. Oh, I would give half my years if the yesterday of life could be blotted out."

She knew that he wished to tell her of the pain which the remembrance of other years—loveless years and years to be forgotten—brought upon him. There, in the silence of the glen, pictures of his past went whirling before his eyes, showing him the scenes he would well have shut out, the burning lips whose kisses he had known, the dark places he had trodden. The girl at his side seemed unreal—a vision from the hills—something beyond his touch or hope. Could he have read her heart he would have known that she was helplessly following the path of her emotions, making no effort to stem the tide of her affection, saying only, "I will lift him up, and in me he shall find all else—even the divine life."

Thus always did the woman in her conquer.

The pause was a long one. He broke it in a sudden memory of the morrow.

"I shall see the king at sunset," he said.

She shuddered.

"And shall carry him your message," he went on.

"And then?"

"Ah! God knows; but in my thoughts I shall be here."

His despondency reminded her again of his danger. She began to tremble for him, telling herself that she had asked the sacrifice.

"You do not fear for yourself?" she asked.

"When I have your friendship."

" But that cannot protect you ;
and the king may yet carry me to the
château."

It was his turn now to anticipate
the shadow upon their path.

" He will never carry you there
while I live," said he.

" Then you have little confidence.
Indeed, *mon ami*, it seems to me that
I shall carry myself to his Majesty to
save you."

" God forbid that such a day
should be !"

She was about to answer him when
the leaves above them rustled, and a
dark figure stood out against the
foliage. Twilight had now come
down into the glen, and darkness almost hid the brook at their feet. So
startling was the apparition—which
was gone in an instant—that the girl
cried out, and instinctively clung to
her companion, who encircled her in
a moment with both his arms, and so
held her close to him. He himself
had seen nothing ; he had heard only
the breaking of the boughs. But to

her the interruption seemed almost a warning.

"Look," said she, "how late it grows. They will be missing us."

"What matter," he cried, "since I have you in my arms."

"I was frightened," she murmured.

"But shall be frightened no more."

She resisted him no longer, and he covered her lips with burning kisses, dismantling her pretty hair so that it was spread about in gold-brown curls upon her shoulders, and holding her so close to him that he could feel the beating of her heart.

"God make me worthy of you," he said—and so he sealed a vow upon her lips.

*   *   *   *

The vesper bell was ringing when they came into the park again, and the masquerade was done. But a group of wise men and chattering hags stood beneath a great gnarled oak, discussing a question of grave import.

"The Little Huguenot."

"God defend us from all evil!" said one of the oracles, "for the spectre monk is abroad in the forest this night."

CHAPTER IX.

PEPIN MAKES A BARGAIN.

DE GUYON rode away from the Château aux Loups at dawn on the morning of the Saturday. It was not until High Mass was done on the Sunday that Gabrielle de Vernet had news of him. At that hour, Pepin the guide came galloping into the courtyard of the château, crying loudly to have audience of its mistress, and of the venerable Abbé who counselled her.

"Mass or no mass," said he to the stableman, "I have a word for them which will not wait, even though I cry it from the pulpit. And hark ye, friend, had'st thou a stoop of wine I would love thee the better. Body of Bacchus, I could drink a river."

The words had scarce left his lips

when the door of the chapel was thrown open, and the deep trumpet-like notes of the great organ filled the courtyard. One by one, the men and women of Gabrielle de Vernet's household passed out to the park, there to greet their neighbours, or to form members of the little groups which discussed this sudden coming of the guide. A few of the older servants waited for their mistress at the door of the church; but she remained some minutes engaged in silent prayer; and when at length she appeared among them, the Abbé Gondy was at her side—a Sabbath smile of generous benevolence upon his face, a great hunger 'for the coming dinner to be read in his watery eyes.

"*Bon jour*, Monsieur Pepin," said the Abbé cheerily when he observed the still-mounted guide, "we did not look for you to-day."

"Nor I for myself, Monsieur l'Abbé," said Pepin, coming down clumsily from his horse; "but what is must be—and that's logic any day.

I have letters for you, my father—
and for my lady here."

The countess had said no word as
yet, but her face had lost the smile it
wore when she had quitted the chapel,
and she answered the buffoon with a
very stately but chilling inclination
of her pretty head.

"You left Monsieur de Guyon
well?" asked the Abbé, looking
wearily at the sealed packet which
had come between him and his dinner.

"*Corbleu!* you jest, monsieur—I
left him in a dungeon, as yonder letter
will tell."

Gabrielle uttered a little cry, but
smothered it on her lips; the Abbé
raised his hands to heaven and rolled
his eyes as though a sharp pain had
cut him.

"God keep us all from harm," said
he, "what a thing to hear!"

"Aye, a sorry tale to come chattering to any house with," added Pepin
apologetically, "and like to be sor-
rier before the week's out. By the

toe of Peter, my poor lieutenant may hear Mass in the Bastille next Sunday."

The girl's heart· was beating very fast while she listened to the news ; tears strove for mastery with her, but were conquered. She was not one to wear her heart upon her sleeve ; and it was with complete self-possession that she spoke to the guide.

" I thank you for your service in this matter," said she, " it was good of you to hasten here. You must now think of dinner and of rest."

" While we find a way of helping our poor friend," murmured the priest.

Leaving Pepin and the Abbé in the court, Gabrielle entered her room, and opened her letter with trembling fingers. When she had read it, she fell upon her knees before the little altar in her oratory, and the tears which she had erstwhile controlled forced themselves through her fingers. She began to reproach herself that she had permitted de Guyon to leave her; she seemed to feel again his burning kisses, but now they stung her lips; she prayed with wild, unchosen words that he might come to her again; she recalled that moment in the park when she lay in his arms —it stood out as the sweetest moment of her life. In spirit she had given herself wholly to the man since that night in the glen. Why, then, she asked bitterly, had she suffered him to go?

Meanwhile the Abbé had taken Pepin to his apartments, and when they were alone, had begun to plague him with a hundred questions.

"You gave the king the packet?" he asked in a low voice.

"Am I then a knave?" pleaded Pepin.

"And his Majesty said—— ?"

"Ah, it was good to hear. He said, 'If that is the face of the little Huguenot, I will ride a hundred leagues to find her.'"

"Merciful God!" cried the Abbé, "he will come here to fetch her."

"It is very possible, my father. That will be a good day for you."

"How—for me?"

"Why, did not I mention it?"

"You said nothing—that's what I complain of, you are a dull fellow."

"Patience, Monsieur l'Abbé," said Pepin, anxious to plan out his tale, "let us first talk about those ten pieces."

"To the devil—that is, you are a greedy rascal."

The Abbé counted the money out upon the table, and then continued impatiently—

"Well—and what now?"

"A cup of the wine of Burgundy, my father." '

The Abbé stamped his foot savagely, but sent for the wine.

"Now," said he, with sarcastic deliberation, "if you do not speak plainly, Monsieur Pepin, I will lay my cudgel on your back."

"The saints forbid that a holy priest should so forget himself. Would you crack the cup to save the wine, monsieur? *Parbleu*, what folly !"

"Then answer me as I wish."

"I am all attention."

"His Majesty referred to his humble servant?"

"Certainly—I have his words in my mind now. 'I shall know how to deal with my friend, the Abbé,' he said ; what more would you want?"

"But that—Holy Virgin, that may mean anything. He would say the same if he sent me to the Bastille."

"Possibly."

"And he added nothing to it?"

"The devil a word."

The Abbé groaned, sinking back in his chair. Pepin continued to quaff huge draughts of the luscious wine, and to plume himself upon the lies he was telling. "Ho, ho," thought he, "the Abbé would cudgel his servant, would he? But we shall see."

"Monsieur Pepin," said the Abbé after a pause, "I am like to come to trouble with the king, I fear. There has been some bungling here. I shall set out for the château this very night, with you for my guide. A word from me will make all straight."

" Aye, that it will."

" You are prepared to accompany me ?"

" My fee is ten crowns, holy father."

The Abbé sighed.

" Very well, then," said he, " I will order the horses for sunset."

CHAPTER X.

THE WOMAN AND THE PRIEST.

GABRIELLE spent the afternoon of her Sunday in prayer and thought. Her young face was deep stained with tears when the vesper bell rang out over the forest ; and for the first time since she had come to the château, the villagers remarked that she was not in church. But she had no heart to appear among them ; and when the sun began to sink over the western woods, she was still pacing her chamber ; at one moment chiding herself for the evil which had befallen ; at the next, taking courage of her impulse to save her lover.

Child that she was, this conviction that she alone could save de Guyon gained strength every hour. It was the one substantial conviction chosen

of all the confusing ideas which came
upon her. Until this time, perhaps,
she had scarce realised that she
loved ; but now passion broke the
bonds, and stood before her question-
ingly. A deep longing to kiss the
lips of her lover again, to stand with
him where he should stand, to suffer
with him when he should suffer, over-
whelmed her. A week ago she would
have laughed to scorn the suggestion
that any man thus should come between her and the path she had
chosen. But destiny was playing
with her ; it remained to be seen if it
would crush her.

Until the dusk fell, she warred with
the many devices which her brain
wrought—rejecting this scheme, dal-
lying with that. Her earliest impulse
had been to write to the king, declar-
ing her love boldly ; concealing nothing in the hope that sincerity would
prove the best of weapons. Anon,
the impossibility of stirring any generous emotions in the heart of the
" Well-Beloved" turned her to

thoughts of her cousin Claude and
of his influence. In any other case,
she said, that influence would help
her ; but what would be its worth
when pitted against the king's will !
Nor had she other kinsman at the
Court, but must come back to the remembrance of her slight relationship
to the Marquis de Monnier, and to
the fact that he was then at Nancy.
The old President would befriend her
if she could gain his ear ; yet how
would de Guyon fare in the between-
while ? Had not Pepin said that he
would be in the Bastille before the
week was out ?

The vesper bell had ceased to boom
in the tower of the chapel ; the chanting of the choir in court and cloister
was like the echo of some sweet celes-
tial hymn ; the cattle in the park
were going down to the waters ; the
birds were roosting, when at length
the mistress of the château made up
her mind. If she had been tempted
at one time to open her heart to the
Abbé, who posed as her governor,

she resolved when dusk had come that she would seek other counsel. The thought had come to her as an inspiration while she had been listening at her window to the music of the choir. In all the country round, she remembered that she had only one friend—and he was an exile and an outcast. But she would go to him in her need, and in his words would find consolation.

Nerved to the resolution by the dominating love which had come so swiftly, so stealthily into her life, she resolved also that she would go alone. Her girlhood shrank from any confidences. If de Guyon were to be saved, it would not be by proclaiming *urbi et orbi* that she loved him. Any sacrifice that she could make she would offer cheerfully. There were wild moments when she said that she would even yield to the king, if thereby she might help her lover ; but this thought she was quick to repent and to beat from her mind. All her purity of soul revolted at it.

She knew that if once Louis's lips touched her own, that never again could she bear de Guyon's kisses, or suffer his embrace.

It was dusk when she took her resolution ; it was nearly dark when at last she quitted the château, hiding her face in the folds of a black cloak, and fleeing with light step to the distant woods. There was not a path in all the forest round that was unfamiliar to her ; scarce a thicket she had not penetrated ; a copse she had not explored. Darkness could not hinder her, nor the shades of night deter. Like some fairy of the glens, she passed now through unfrequented meadows ; now through ravines hid in the darkness ; now by black pools and bubbling streamlets. Often she would pause to listen to the snapping of the twigs or the rustle of the branches—but her ear told her that no human thing was near. She walked alone—a worthy child of the forest she loved.

Once in her flight, she passed the

hut of some woodlanders who had grouped themselves about a fire of logs. They started up with oaths upon their lips when they heard her footstep ; but observing her young face, they crossed themselves and called upon the saints. Or, again, she came of a sudden upon a rough fellow, a worthy tenant of the Caverne des Brigands, which she was approaching ; and for a moment a savage thought possessed him, and he made a step towards her. But she looked him full in the face, and recognising her, he slunk away into the bramble like a boy that has been beaten. The little Huguenot was not as other women to such a one ; she was a child of mystery, a guardian spirit breathing benevolence and charity and love ; a creature of the heavens sent to do battle with devils stalking the forest. There was not a woodlander about the precincts of the château who did not in some way associate her with the Blessed Virgin. They called her sometimes a " daughter of Mary." And this was rather the outcome of their love than of their ignorance.

At the distance of half-a-mile or less from that dark place of the forest known as the Cave of the Brigands, Gabrielle began for the first time to find trouble of the way. She was now in the heart of an almost impenetrable wood, a wood where thorn and briar were knitted about the serried trunks, and sweet-smelling creepers twined ropes across her path. So heavy was the canopy of branches, so close did the bushes grow, that the dark of a moonless night reigned in all the grove. Even the cloudless sky above was hidden by the leaves ; no path trodden of man was to be seen ; the only note upon the silence was the ceaseless music of the nightingale, or the howling of the wolves. And through this wood, onward to its depths, the girl must pick her steps ; often tearing her arms in the bramble, often feeling some beast or bird stirring at her very feet, often despairing of her mission.

In the heart of the grove, and when Gabrielle had told herself that she had mistaken the way and must retrace her steps, she came suddenly upon a little lawn of grass, and at this she cried aloud with pleasure. Hid in the trees upon the opposite side of the sward was a hut of logs, from the open door of which an aureole of light fell upon the grass, shining as a beacon of the wood warningly. And the girl's cry was heard and answered ; scarce had it escaped her lips when the outcast Jesuit, who had warned de Guyon as he went to the château, stood in the doorway of the hut asking, " Who goes ?"

" It is I, Gabrielle," she said, trembling in spite of herself.

" Merciful God, you !" cried the priest, holding his lantern high, that its rays might fall upon her face.

" Yes," she said, recovering her calm when she heard his voice ; " I come to you for help—you will not refuse it to me ?"

" I, child—what a thought !"

She followed him into the hut, which contained little but his bed of moss, his books of devotion, and his crucifix. She knew nothing of the devils tearing at the man's heart, of the hours when her face had stood between him and his prayers, when he had wrestled with her haunting image until the sweat stood upon his brow. To her, he was one of God's messengers—a man between whose soul and sin a great gulf was fixed. And while she offered him this whole worship of her trust, voices were crying in his ears and telling him that he loved her.

But while all this was passing in his mind he had found a log for her to sit upon, and setting the lantern between them, he fixed his questioning eyes upon her.

" My child," he said, " you are in trouble ?"

She answered him very simply, tell-

ing him of the coming of the king's
messenger, and of his arrest. But of
her love, she had not as yet the courage to speak. Nor did the priest
read her heart, as she looked for him
to do.

" Well," said he, when he had
thought long upon the matter, " and
what is all this to you ? The man
came here with lies upon his lips.
Why should you stand between him
and his intrigues ?"

" What he suffers, he suffers for
me," she pleaded.

" Nay ; what he suffers, he suffers
for his ambition."

" But he carried my message."

" Which you have no proof that he
delivered."

" I have his promise and I ask no
more. Oh, you do not know him as
I do !"

The priest raised his eyes quickly.

" You come here as his friend,
then——"

" I come here to save him."

" But why ?—what is he to you ?"

"He—he is my lover."

She had not thought that it would
be so difficult to tell him, but now
when the word was spoken her heart-
strings were unloosed, and she continued passionately—

"Judge me not hastily, my father
—only pray for me. I am a woman
and I have a woman's heart. If I
love, it is because my heart bids me
to love. Indeed, it is not given us to
say yes or no. A week ago, I believed that I should live alone always
for Christ and His glory, but this has
come into my life as a gift of God.
Oh, I cannot turn from it, I cannot
make myself other than I am."

The priest's hands were clenched,
there was a strange buzzing in his
ears, his brain seemed to burn while
he listened to her words. He had
been in some way the master of himself so long as she lived the virgin's
life at the château ; but now that she
talked of love for another man, a
fierce, passionate envy came upon
him, and there was a moment when

his strength seemed to ebb so that he could scarce wrestle longer with temptation.

" You forsake, then," he said sternly, " the faith to which Christ has called you ; you thrust from you the companionship of the saints ; you close your ears to the heavenly voices——"

She fell upon her knees before him sobbing.

" No, no !" she exclaimed ; " I forsake nothing as God is my witness —I only love."

He raised her up with a gentle hand. The generosity of his soul was prevailing over his humanity.

" My child," he said, " who am I to be your judge—or to say this is or this is not the will of God. May His Holy Spirit guide you !"

With this word, he knelt at his faldstool ; and while she believed that he was offering a prayer for her, he warred anew with the impulses which possessed him, suffered all the agony of a soul in bondage. When he rose up at last, his eyes were full of kindness for her, and the touch of her hand no longer thrilled him.

"Come," said he, "you have not yet told me how I am to help you."

She looked up into his face and answered him frankly—

"Bring my lover to me."

She believed that he was all-powerful, a man above men, whose word was a command, whose will might work miracles. And he, knowing his weakness, was yet vain of her confidence.

"I—child," said he, "for whose body there is a ransom ; I, whom the king would tear limb from limb ; how shall I bring your lover back to you ?"

"I cannot answer you. I have no other friend—I trust you. You will not let me suffer."

He was standing at the door of his hut now, and before he spoke again, he paced the grassy knoll which was his garden. The moon had risen above the forest while they talked, and all the woods were lit with the silver beams. There was exhilaration in the night-air ; a breath of courage and of strength.

"Gabrielle," said the priest, waking suddenly from the spell which the beauties of the night had cast upon him, "is the king at his château ?"

"He was there at dawn."

"Who brought the news ?"

"Pepin, the guide."

"He carried a letter for the Abbé ?"

"Yes."

"Ah !"

He stood for a moment erect, the moon shining upon his black hair, his eyes looking fondly upon the girl at his side.

"Child," said he, "there is but one way out of your difficulty—you must see the king."

"See him !"

"As I say, you must leave here at dawn and go straight to the château of Francis."

"But—oh my father—you know
that he has sent for me."

"I know all; that is why I wish
you to see him."

"And when I am there?"

"When you are there, I shall be
there too."

"You—but they would kill you."

The Jesuit laughed a little bitterly.

"They have long asked my death,"
said he, "and yet I live. Fear nothing for me."

Selfishness is often the dominating
note of love. Gabrielle heard in the
priest's words only the promise that
he would save de Guyon. And so
great was her trust in this man's
strength, that all her trouble seemed
over when he bade her follow him to
her home. She did not know, as she
watched him striding along with the
lantern's light dancing on their path,
that he was thinking of Damiens,
who had been torn limb from limb
by wild horses. So also would they
do to him when the king's men laid
hands upon him.

CHAPTER XI.

THE ABBÉ AND THE TREE.

WHILE the Jesuit was guiding Gabrielle through the labyrinthine way of the woods, Pepin was reckoning with himself on a hill-top in that part of the forest known as the desert.

" God deliver me from all abbés !" said he ruefully ; and then with unction in his voice he began to cry loudly—

" This way, Monsieur l'Abbé, this way. Guardian angels keep your holy feet out of yonder bog. *Dieu !* I thought that I had lost you."

Now the Abbé's feet were not holy ; they were only swollen with the gout ; Pepin knew well enough that the venerable man was not lost. The truth was that the artful guide found himself in such a pretty net, that he had led the priest three good leagues out of his way, while he himself re-considered his position. "For," said he, "if I carry this Abbé to the palace, the king will learn that I have been lying; or again, if I carry him back to the château, he will want his ten crowns of me. *Corbleu!* I must think of it."

The Abbé's mule came labouring up the hill, and presently the corpu-lent body of the Churchman was to be observed in the moonlight. His face was scarlet with passion, and with the wounds which the thorns had cut in his skin.

"Fool and knave," cried he to Pe-pin, "that makes pretence to be a guide, and yet cannot lead me six leagues through the forest. By the God above me, I will crack my staff upon your back if you do not find the path this instant."

Pepin shrugged his shoulders.

"Look you, my father," said he, "what an ill thing that would be—for the instant is already gone, and we are not come to the path. Did you crack your staff, there would be one good cudgel less in the world, and, like enough, no master for it when the morning came. Oh, we are in a pretty place! Body of Paul, I am near to being lost as ever I was."

"Lost!" gasped the Abbé, "then the Lord help us. Do you dare to tell me that you know nothing of this road?"

Pepin scratched his head.

"Yonder," said he, "lies the brigands' den, as full of cut-throats as a nest of eggs. Yonder again"—and here he swept his arm round bravely, indicating the wood they were about to enter—"is the very tree upon which they hanged the body of the Chevalier Geoffrin after they had robbed him of his purse and cut off his hands. Turn where you will, my father, you may pick up assassins like pebbles in a river's bed. Aye, it is a pretty place—a place for prayer and not for jest."

___

Beads of perspiration gathered thick upon the Abbé's brow; his hands trembled so that he could not finger his rosary.

"Good Pepin," said he, "you are my friend; I have confidence in you, Pepin; you will lead me out of this."

"Aye, though Beelzebub himself stood in the path. Courage, Monsieur l'Abbé, do you hear the wolves —*Dieu*, what throats they have!"

Pepin had more than a suspicion that "the wolves" were only watchdogs howling at the moon, but he saw no reason to enlighten the now trembling Abbé. For the matter of that, he had little stomach himself for the ugly copse which they were entering; and would have given a half of his wage to have been in his bed again. He had spoken no more than the truth when he said that the near woods were a haven for cutthroats and brigands; and guide that he was, he would not willingly have fallen into their hands. Truly, this

lumbering Abbé was a burden to
him ; nor could he at the first think
of any plan by which he might rid
himself of his company. And still
thinking upon it, he plunged into
the darkness of the copse.

" Oh blessed Thaddeus, Linus,
Cletus, Clement, Xystus, Cornelius,
pray for me this night !" murmured
the Abbé, while his mule stumbled
in the dark place, and the hoofs of
the beast squelched in the mud of
the bog. " Merciful Heaven, that I
should have left my bed for this !"

" Aye, that's it," chimed in Pepin,
" if we had not left our beds ! God
knows where, we shall next stretch
ourselves—in yonder bog, perchance,
if your saints are sleeping. And we
shall have company too, my father.
Did you hear that cry ? Put me in
the pillory if that was the night
bird's voice."

" Then what was it, Pepin ?"

" *Corbleu !* what was it ? Some
devil of the woods abroad for all I
know. Oh, it is a pretty place."

The Abbé's teeth were chattering audibly ; the cold had chilled his very marrow ; the mud was thick upon his cassock ; his face was blue and bleeding.

" Pepin," said he at last in his desperation, " lead me to some house. I can go no further. I care not where it is, or in whose company I lie. Take me where you will. I must sleep."

He spoke in a voice pitiful enough to have drawn tears from the rock ; but the cunning guide had no heart for his situation. Pepin heard only an appeal which gave him an excuse for turning once more from the way ; and the opportunity fell in well with his plans.

" To a house, my father ! Oh, you could ask me nothing that I would do so gladly. To a house ! Mother of God, I know an honest fellow not half a league from here who will answer to our knock with a bed of moss and a cup of wine which a prince bishop might drink. Courage,

monsieur, courage ! You are at the
end of your troubles. Once past
yonder copse, wherein there may lie
perhaps a hundred rogues, to say
nothing of the wolves, I will venture
my head on your safety. Only have
a little patience."

He turned his horse quickly at the
saying, but so clumsy was the move-
ment that his lantern was extinguished by it ; and there was now
but one light remaining. The wood
to which they had come was like a
patch of virgin forest, a maze of
climbing plant and creeper, of black-
thorn and briar, of bog and bramble.
So thick was the undergrowth that
man might have been treading it for
the first time ; so black were the
pools that they seemed to be the
waste waters of Styx-like rivers, hidden in the caverns below the hills.
Game swarmed here ; boars crashed
through the branches ; foxes sneaked
across the bridle-path ; birds, dis-
turbed at roost, rose up with hissing
cries and loud flapping of their wings.

"The Little Huguenot."

Over all was the intense darkness of the forest, night at her zenith, the supremity of solitude and of nature.

Any other man but Pepin would have been lost beyond hope in this labyrinth; but the guide knew the forest as he knew his own face. The very darkness of the way inspired him. He turned gaily from the path he had struck at the first, and riding as it were straight towards a gloomy bog whose shallow waters caught a leaden glow of the moon's beams, he encouraged the bewildered Abbé to new efforts.

"Well done, monsieur, well done," he cried; "a half a league ridden like that and you shall smack your lips over a wine-cup. Oh, was there ever such an idea! That you should ask me to lead you to a house! Blood of the martyrs, you bear yourself bravely."

"Is it very far, Pepin?" asked the Abbé, in a very weak voice.

"The matter of a league and a half, as I told you, my father."

" You said half-a-league, rascal,"
cried the Abbé.

" What, do you think that I lie ?"
exclaimed Pepin, stopping his horse
suddenly.

" The good God forbid," stammered the Abbé ; " only take me to a
house, and I will forgive you all."

Pepin was not to be appeased so
easily.

" Hark ye, Monsieur l'Abbé," said
he, " another word like that and
I leave you to pace the three
leagues——"

" Three leagues, *ciel !*"

" As I said—three leagues. If you
know the road so well, my father, I
will even follow the path at your
mule's tail."

The Abbé shivered at the idea.

" Saints and angels soften the
heart of this guide," he muttered.

They had now come to the slope of
the wood upon the border of the
dirty bog. Pepin's horse, which had
trodden the path often, went down
fearlessly to the water, but the Abbé's

mule was in no mood for the venture, jibbing at it and sliding down at length with his forefeet set out as an advance guard.

"This way, Monsieur l'Abbé, this way," cried Pepin; "oh, what a beast to carry the body of a holy priest. I would not hire him for a German mountebank. The ford is here, my father. Oh, have a care!"

The warning was well meant, but too late to be of any service to the Abbé, whose mule tripped suddenly upon the edge of the black ditch and shot its rider far out into the stream. For one long minute the Abbé floundered wildly in the mud. Then he snatched at the low branch of an overhanging oak—and so drew himself up, all bedraggled and half-suffocated, to a haven of refuge among the boughs.

"Pepin, Pepin!" he gasped; "oh, help me! I am dying, Pepin! *Dieu*, what cold, what suffering!"

But Pepin was already riding away

through the wood on the opposite bank.

"Patience, a little patience, holy father," cried he, "I go to get help; the good God guard you until I return."

"May all the devils of hell go with you!" shouted the Abbé.

And thus it was that when dawn came, a forester observed the strange spectacle of a venerable Abbé saying his prayers in the bough of a tree.

CHAPTER XII.

DE GUYON HEARS THE NEWS.

THE king had been at the château of Francis two days without making up his mind about de Guyon. It was the evening of Monday, and he had put the lieutenant under arrest at midnight on Saturday ; being then much troubled at the letter which the Abbé Gondy had sent to him, and not at all sure what lay behind the musketeer's duplicity. " Fie !" said he, " I will bring this little witch to the palace though I carry her, as she asks ; and as for this booby, if he has been making love to her, I will hang him."

Worn by thirty years of uninter-rupted debauchery, grown feeble, seeking new pleasures for a jaded ap-petite, easily provoked to anger or to suspicion, roundly hated in all France, the "Well-Beloved" was in no mood to bear with any patience the affront which had been put upon him. For more than a year now, the strange creed, in some part Protestant, in some part Republican, in some part ascetic, which Gabrielle de Vernet had preached at the Château aux Loups had been a by-word and a jest among the wits of the Court. The amiable Madame de Boufflers had risen to her finest flights of humour when discussing it ; Madame Doublet de Persan had died with a lie about it on her lips. While, on the one hand, the evil-minded shrugged their shoulders, evilly implying that something more than mere spirituality lay behind the asceticism of the little Huguenot ; on the other hand were many to whisper in the king's ear tales of the fascination which she exercised upon those about her, and of the indisputable beauty of which she was the possessor. Goaded by the incessant chatter to the point of ac-

tive curiosity, Louis had determined
to see the girl for himself, and to
hear from her own lips that apocalypse with which the people cred-
ited her. No doubt he contemplated
with content the subjection of so
much morality and vaunted righteousness to the perils of the Court ;
no doubt his real purpose was deep,
and linked closely to his lust. In
any case, it boded no good to her
most concerned, nor was it made
weaker by her obstinacy. "I will
send a troop of horse for her, and
burn her chapel about her ears," he
cried once in a rage. Sixty years of
life had not taught him patience.

In truth, it was Gabrielle de Vernet's refusal that set the fires of
smouldering passion aflame. He
said that she should boast of her
righteousness no longer ; should become the sport of those very men and
women at whom she had pointed her
finger. And if she had thoughts of
the lieutenant who had so bungled
his duty, he would know how to con-

duct the affair to a pretty conclusion.
In which spirit, he kept de Guyon a
prisoner in a sunless room near the
Cour Ovale, and denied to him even
an account of that crime which had
robbed him in a moment of his sword
and of his love-dreams.

On the morning of the Monday,
Louis rode abroad in the forest in
the company of the Grand Falconer,
the Comte de Vaudreuil, and of the
Grand Louvetier, the Comte d'Haus-
sonville. He had come to the palace
quite privately, consoling himself
with the hope that the little Huguenot would be there to amuse him ;
and in her absence he found that
time was his enemy. Indeed, he
spoke of returning to Versailles on
the following morning, saying to
himself that Gabrielle de Vernet
should be brought there publicly as a
part of her punishment. At the
same time, he would sign the *lettre de
cachet* which should send his amorous
lieutenant to For-l'Evêque, where he
would have the leisure to consider

what sort of a bargain he had made
for himself.

Early in the afternoon, the king
dined privately, discarding here any
of that publicity which he observed
unfailingly at Versailles. He went
afterwards to the orangery, and to
the park, remaining abroad nearly
until sunset. Meanwhile, de Guyon
paced the dingy room in the Cour
Ovale ; now permitting himself to
hope, now abandoning himself to the
gloomy possibilities which crowded
upon his mind. Nor could the honest fellow, his servant Antoine, in
any way lead him to that sensible dis-
cussion of his position which alone
might lead to his liberation. It
seemed to him that fate had opened
his eyes to the sweet vision of Gabrielle but to plague him ; had permitted him to dream, that the awakening
might be more bitter. In the solitude of confinement, he recalled her
words, her humours, her angers, her
prettiness. He remembered that the
touch of her hand had sent fire leap-

ing through his veins; he dwelt on
that moment when he had held her
in his arms and had known the supreme ecstasy of life. Yet all this
was of the past. What the morrow
would be, God alone could tell.

Towards evening, when the old
oaks were casting lengthening shadows upon the lawns by the lake, and
the fish-pond shone like a burnished
mirror, and all the statues seemed to
sleep, a sudden palaver and commo-
tion in the court without recalled
him from his visions to the realities
in the Château de Fontainebleau.
He thought at the first that they had
come to take him to For-l'Evêque or
even to the Bastille, and thus to end
for many years the hopes which he
treasured so diligently. He knew
that the king gave short shrift to
those who stood between him and his
pleasures. He had seen many an
honest man snatched from life by
the "Well-Beloved's" caprice; had
watched the quick degradation of
many a woman who had withstood

his desires. And he had begun to believe that Louis had never set himself to any purpose with more determination than to his ensnarement of Gabrielle de Vernet.

From the narrow windows of his room in the White Tower, he could see nothing of that which was happening in the courtyard of the château. But he heard the clatter of hoofs upon the stone pavement, and his servant, Antoine, came in presently looking like one who has news upon his tongue. Scarce had he passed the door when de Guyon began to question him.

"Has the king returned, Antoine?"

"*Ma foi*, no," replied the other.

"He is still riding, then?"

"He is in the orangery with the Comte de Buffon."

"Then whose horses do I hear?"

Antoine, who loved the lieutenant and guessed how things stood with him, avoided the question.

"There is talk of his Majesty riding away to-morrow," said he.

"Ah !" exclaimed de Guyon. "Then I shall know to-morrow what he has in store for me."

"A month in For-l'Evêque at the most, *mon maître*—at least, that is the gossip of the gallery."

De Guyon shrugged his shoulders.

"And after that, Antoine ?"

"Your sword and, perhaps, a command. The king has not a long memory, monsieur !"

"You think so ?"

"I have no doubt of it ; and now that madame has come here, he will soon wish her at the château again."

"Madame ! to whom do you refer ?"

"Then you have not heard. Madame de Vernet rode into the courtyard half-an-hour ago."

De Guyon swung round upon his heel, and faced his servant.

"Antoine," cried he, "what tale is this ?"

"Tale, *mon maître ?*"

"Certainly, as I say—what does it mean ?"

"It is no tale ; madame arrived at the château as I came by the Salle des Gardes."

"You do not jest with me ?"

"I—jest ? God forbid !"

"Then she is here ?"

"Without doubt she is."

"And the king knows of her coming ?"

"They say that he will sup with her to-night."

"They lie ! I will prevent her."

"You ! Oh, but you forget ; there is a guard at your door."

De Guyon sank upon a bench and buried his face in his hands. The idol he had raised up seemed to come crashing headlong to the ground. It were as if Gabrielle had been torn from his arms in that moment ; had been snatched from him while her kisses were still warm upon his lips. When Antoine spoke to him again, there were tears in his eyes.

"Courage, my master ; these Huguenots are all alike," cried the honest fellow ; "their virtue would not fill a nut. *Diable!* They have the clothes of a nun and the heart of a grisette! What a pity that you should trouble yourself with their affairs."

De Guyon did not answer him. He was wrestling silently with his overwhelming despair — contrasting the Gabrielle of the Château aux Loups with the woman who of her own will had come to sup with the king at Fontainebleau. There was a time when he had said that he was not worthy to raise her hand to his lips. What a fool he had been to believe in her pretty platitudes! She was as the others—not better, no worse. And yet the memory of that moment when he had held her in his arms was not to be blotted out. He would have given half the years remaining to him to know that the news which Antoine brought was false. There were even prayers upon his lips for her by whom he had been taught to pray.

CHAPTER XIII.

THE news that Gabrielle de Vernet had presented herself at the palace was brought to the king when he was with Buffon in the orangery. He heard it with a laugh that was half a sneer; and yet with no little satisfaction.

"Ha!" said he, "so we shall not have to carry the little witch through the forest. That booby of a lieutenant has been lying to me. I shall know how to settle his affair."

The reflection was pleasing to him. Of all hurts, Louis resented most any hurt to his dignity, and he could but regard this sudden face about as a direct act of homage from a pretty woman.

"You have conducted madame to her apartment?" he asked.

"She is lodged above the Porte
Dorée, sire."

"That is well done, we shall sup
there—let the orders for to-morrow
be cancelled. We shall rest here
some days."

The man withdrew, and the "Well-
Beloved" returned to his apartments
in the Salle des Chasses. The coming of the little Huguenot had altered
all his plans, and blotted from his
mind that resentment he felt towards
her. She would amuse him, at any
rate, he said, and it would be a new
thing to make love to a woman who
had professed piety and a certain
vague but polite republicanism. He
could find in' the fact of her arrival
nothing but the surrender of herself
to his wish, the abnegation of that
creed which had made the Château
aux Loups so fine a theme of mockery
at the palace. And being beyond all
things a vain man, his vanity was fed
by this conquest of scruples, as it had
never been fed by all the debaucheries
of an infamous life.

" The Little Huguenot."

It was full dusk when Gabrielle
found herself at last in her chamber
above the Porte Dorée. She had
been lodged in the suite of rooms
which adjoined the apartments at one
time occupied by Madame de Main-
tenon ; and to these she came when
the last shimmer of the sun had vanished from the lake, and the first
breath of night stirred the great oaks
in the park. Though she bore herself bravely, wearing that happy
smile which was the fairest emblem
of her girlhood, none the less did her
courage often fail her as she realised
her environment and the unspeakable
dangers into which she had plunged.
There were moments when she re-
proached herself in that she had listened to the Jesuit, and had staked
all upon this throw ; other moments
when she asked if such a love as she
felt for de Guyon was not in itself an
unholy thing, a concession to the humanity in her, and a negation to those
high spiritual ideals she had served.
She feared in some vague way that

her presence at Fontainebleau would
make her unworthy of the man for
whom she had dared so much ; she
shuddered when she remembered
that she must meet the king presently, and that she was alone. She
had seen nothing of the Jesuit since
he had left her at the gates of her
own home. She had come to Fontainebleau with her old servant,
Dominique, and four lusty yeomen
for escort. But these were now
lodged in another court of the palace ; the rooms she occupied were
full of gaudy splendours, yet of suggestions of isolation and of loneliness.
Her quick imagination peopled them
with spectres of the past—with the
shapes of the men and women who
had enjoyed here their brief hours
of indulgence and of pleasure. She
heard in fancy the laughter of the
dead ; the cries of those who had
suffered haunted her ; turn where
she would the air seemed full of
warnings.

With such fancies was her brain

busy ; but to Dominique, observing
her closely and troubled by many ap-
prehensions, she betrayed none of
her fears. Watch her as he would,
he was confronted only by the Gabrielle of the château, by the Gabrielle of the masks and fêtes, of the
hard rides and the merry picnics in
the woods. It may have been that
he would have seen her rather as the
Gabrielle of the chapel and the devout retreat ; but it was something
to know that she had lost nothing of
her courage, that the mistress of the
Château aux Loups would carry herself well, even before the king. With
which thought, the old man lit the
candles in the great gilt scones, and
began to draw the curtains over the
long windows. He felt that he alone
was there to protect her, and he
would do his duty.

" My lady will wish to rest until
supper is served ?" he asked.

" Indeed, no, Dominique, my lady
would very much like to know where
she is first."

" Is she not in the Château de Fontainebleau ?"

" Assuredly, she is in the Château de Fontainebleau, though when that is said, she is still very ignorant Look you, Dominique, was there ever a passage with so many doors, or a room so dark ? I am sure this must be the place where Monaldeschi died. There are ghosts in the air."

She shuddered visibly. The old man crossed himself, and drew the curtains.

" We are on a strange errand," said he ; " God send us home again without hurt."

Gabrielle said nothing. She was thinking how full of gloom the room was, now that it was lit by the flickering light of tapers.

" Dominique," cried she, after a pause, " you gave them my message, that I would be served here only by you ?"

" Certainly, my lady."

" And they said——"

" That your wish was the king's while you were in the château."

She laughed a little ironically ; and standing by one of the curtains he had drawn, she began to play with the tassel of it. The next question that she set the old man was put in hesitation—

"Dominique," she asked, "have you heard of my friend Monsieur de Guyon ?"

"Truly, I have ; he is the king's guest in an apartment not a hundred paces from here."

"And they do not speak of the king's intention to send him away ?"

"The talk is that he leaves at daybreak for a lodging in For-l'Evêque."

"We have come in time. Think you, Dominique, that it would be strange if the king changed his mind ?"

He raised his eyes quickly to hers.

"He will change it if madame wills."

"And I am going to do so."

Dominique shook his head.

"She is blind, and she is a child,"

he said to himself ; " may God help us this night."

" You have learnt nothing of Père Cavaignac since you have been here ?" continued the girl after another pause in which the old man kept his eyes steadily upon her.

" *Ma foi !* of Père Cavaignac. Do you not know that it would be death to him to show his face ?"

" Yet he will come."

" He will come ! *Dieu !* you believe that ?"

" As I believe that you are talking to me."

" And you are relying on his help ?"

" Entirely—he is my only friend."

Dominique turned on his heel with an abruptness foreign to his usual deference. " This craze of hers has made her mad," said he ; " God forgive me for setting out on such an affair."

Craze or no craze, Gabrielle continued to believe that the Jesuit would come to her help. Whence,

or by what means or at what moment, she knew not ; none the less
did she hope. Never in her life had
she appealed to him in vain ; never
had she heard of one whom he had
refused to befriend. Almost her
earliest memories were those of the
glades of the forest which this strange
mystic used to roam. She remembered his surpassing love for children, his gentleness, his unceasing
devotion. When she was a child,
she had accounted it a great day if
she might spend the hours in his
company ; when she had come to
womanhood she was uplifted by his
word and his example, made strong
in his strength. There had been no
trouble of hers which he had not
shared ; no joy at which he had not
rejoiced. And he had not rebuked
now when this new love had come
into her life, this quick conquering
passion for one of whom she knew
nothing but that she loved him.
Nay, he had bidden her go to the
palace, had told her that where she

was there would he be also. She believed his word—and this was well,
since upon it alone was her hope
built. To no other at Fontainebleau
could she appeal ; never was a woman more utterly alone.

This sense of loneliness was, in
truth, her despair as the minutes
passed and the moment for the king's
coming approached. Though she
had regarded Louis's intention to
sup with her as an adventure which
should provoke laughter rather than
alarm, the presence of lackeys, who
began to set the table for the repast,
recalled to her the reality of it all,
and perhaps the danger. If the
Jesuit was not to fail her, at any rate
he had long deferred his coming. It
was then half-past seven, and the
king was to sup with her at eight ;
she began to contemplate the possibility of having to bear the whole
brunt of his company ; of having to
defend herself in an encounter which
many an older woman might have

dreaded. The thought of de Guyon alone nerved her to the idea. She had come to Fontainebleau for love of him—for love of him would she combat all the shame that might be put upon her.

Soon after her arrival at the palace, she had changed her riding-dress of green for a black gown, decked out with lace at the throat and arms, but sombre when contrasted with the gaudy splendours about her. Her only ornament was a little diamond cross upon her breast ; but her beauty was enhanced by the simplicity, and it stood out radiantly when she appealed to Dominique at a quarter to eight, the smile still about her lips, but her hands trembling beyond concealment.

" You have no news of Père Cavaignac yet ?" she asked.

" You still believe that he will come, my lady ?"

She had begun to doubt, but of her doubts she would not speak.

"Of course he will come!" she said in a low voice. "Has he not promised me?"

"*Parbleu!* and you think that he would show his face in the king's palace. *Ma foi*, what an idea!"

"I have no doubt that he will find a way. He knows this château as no other man knows it. There is not a room of which he has not the secrets. Oh, I am sure that he will find a way, Dominique."

"And if he does?"

"I shall have a friend."

"Whom the guard will seize so soon as he opens his lips to declare himself. A pretty friend, my lady."

She had not thought of this—of the weakness of the priest wearing the mantle of strength in her presence, because of that child-like belief of which she was the victim. But when the old servant spoke of it, the scales fell from her eyes, and for the first time she became conscious of her own helplessness.

"Dominique!" she exclaimed,

"I have done wrong in coming here."

"As I said upon the way, madame."

If he had offered to her any sympathy, or had spoken a comforting word, perchance her courage would have stood strong to the encounter; but he remembered only that an unreasoning impulse had brought her to the palace, and that she must pay the penalty. In which mood he fell to his work again, and she was left in the great room, with her loneliness and her fears for company. Then, for the first time, there were tears in her eyes, and she fell upon her knees in the dark alcove of the window, to pray that strength might be given to her.

Though the neighbouring room was lit by the light of a hundred tapers, and the mirrors caught up and scattered the bountiful rays, her own apartment had been left almost in darkness. She heard no longer the buzz of lackeys' voices or the

ringing of glasses ; yet she could
smell the perfume of the roses upon
the table, and she knew that supper
was served, and that any minute
might bring her face to face with the
man who was moved by no impulse
but the impulse of his pleasure ; who
had never spoken a noble word, or
done an unselfish deed. The reality
fed the fears which now possessed
her ; she could have cried aloud for
pity and for help ; she thought even
of flight, yet remembered her lover
and prayed the more. And her an-
guish was at the zenith when the answer came.

Swift and sudden the apparition
was, coming like a phantom out of
the shadows of the room. She heard
no step ; no door turned upon its
hinges ; no footfall broke the silence ;
yet was she conscious that one stood
beside her, that his eyes were watching her, that her faith was justified.
Without a word, she turned to him ;
the tears she had conquered gushed
forth again and fell upon his out-

---

stretched hand ; she clung to him like a child that has found a father.

"I knew you would come to me," she cried at last.

" And I am here, my child."

" You will not leave me now ?"

" Leave you—God forbid !"

" And you will help my lover ?"

" I come to set him free."

She would have thanked him, but he raised his hand warningly, while in the court without a bell began to strike the hour.

" Hark !" said he, " that is eight o'clock. There is no time for words. Do only that which I bid you."

He stepped to the oaken wall upon the opposite side of the room, and pressing his hand upon the glass of a small mirror, he opened a panel in the wainscoting, and beckoned to her.

" Three doors from here to the right is the chapel of St. Louis. Wait there until you are summoned."

The girl saw nothing but a dark and gloomy passage, but she went readily at his words, and when the echo of her steps had died away he closed the panel. At the same moment, the door in the second chamber was shut gently.

The " Well-Beloved" had come to sup.

CHAPTER XIV.

THE Jesuit wore his cassock, and a black cape about his shoulders. His step was like the step of a cat, as he crossed the room and stooped in the shadow of an angle, wherefrom he could observe the king. Never in his life had he embarked upon a venture of which the outcome was so doubtful ; never had he more need of his mind and of his courage. One cry uttered by Louis, one false step of his own, and the end would be swift. He stood alone to fight the battle of the woman ; and even while he waited he remembered that the flesh of Damiens had been torn with red-hot pincers, that the body of Ravaillac had been burst asunder to make a Parisian holiday.

Motionless, his body bent forward, his right hand raised, his left hand closed upon the hilt of a dagger, the priest watched the king. The "Well-Beloved," uncertain as he may have been of the welcome which Gabrielle de Vernet would give to him, had determined that there should be no spectator of it. His few attendants had left him at the end of the gallery which gave access to the Salles des Chasses. The lackeys had done their work when they had spread the table. There was only the old man Dominique in the chamber, and he was dismissed with a word. Louis thought himself to be quite alone, and in this expectation he entered the supper-room with a brisk step.

He had expected to find Gabrielle de Vernet waiting there to receive him, and when he beheld the empty room, he stood for a moment uncertain how to act. Old as he was and wildly as he had lived, he yet preserved that superb dignity of bearing which had been his one merit for more than twenty years. It was possible still to speak of him as a handsome man ; and now when the light fell full upon his coat of white and silver, and the jewels upon his vest gave back radiating beams, there was an air of kingship and of grace about him which was an ill contrast to the purpose of his coming.

Standing for a spell by the brilliantly-lighted table, the king listened for any sound or sign of the woman from whom he had expected greeting. When none was given to him, a curious smile began to play upon his face, and he crossed to the door of the inner room, peering into the gloom of it.

" The little witch is pleased to play with me," he muttered ; " well, the game is amusing, and we shall see."

The smile left his face, and he puckered up his lips, biting them while he debated upon the situation. So close to the priest was he then that he could have touched him with his hand ; but he had eyes only for the aureole of light in the centre of the apartment, and at that he gazed while a minute passed. At the end of that time he snapped his fingers as though an idea had come to him, and began to cross the room. The priest stepped noiselessly from the angle and followed him.

Quite convinced now that if he would sup with Gabrielle de Vernet he must carry her to the table, as she had asked, the king crossed the second of the rooms with quick steps, and began to knock upon the panel. He was answered almost at the first rap, but it was the mocking voice of Père Cavaignac which he heard.

" Enter, sire," said the priest.

Louis turned upon his heel at the words, and faced the Jesuit. A flush of passion was upon his face, an oath upon his lips.

" Blood of the Sacrament, who are you ?" he asked.

The priest opened his cape and stepped into the light.

"The Little Huguenot."

"I am the servant of Jesus, François Cavaignac, at one time known to your Majesty."

There were few of the Bourbons that lacked courage, and the "Well-Beloved" was not among their number. Though the presence of the Jesuit had already struck him chill with a fear he could not define, he betrayed himself in no way.

"Well," said he with a fine smile of irony, "and what does the servant of Jesus, François Cavaignac, want with me?"

The priest advanced a step.

"The liberty of a prisoner, sire."

Louis retreated as the other advanced until, when he answered, his back was against the door upon which he had knocked.

"Ha!" he cried, "the liberty of a prisoner. And his name is—— ?"

"A lieutenant of your Majesty's Musketeers, Paul de Guyon."

The king's face flushed with passion; the hand of the other was trembling beneath his robe.

"Dog of a priest," snarled Louis, "I will have you hanged upon the nearest tree."

"Possibly," said the priest in a cold, clear voice, "but your Majesty would be the first to die."

"How—you threaten me?"

"Decidedly—since you compel it."

The king sank into a chair with great drops of perspiration upon his face. The priest stood immovable, motionless. There was silence between them for many minutes, but Louis was the first to speak again.

"Come," said he, "you are a pretty jester, friend. Do you know that I can have you torn limb from limb by a word spoken from those windows?"

"You will never speak it, sire."

"Indeed, but it shall be spoken now."

He rose from his chair, but had not made a step when the hand of the ecclesiastic closed upon his arm with an iron grip.

"Your Majesty wishes still to live?"

"I?"

"Then do not call the guard."

"What—you proclaim yourself to be an assassin?"

"As you please—I say, do not call the guard to find your body here."

The king sank back into the chair trembling in all his limbs; but the priest went on with his words.

"Sire," said he, "if you fear, you fear because of yourself. Give me this man's freedom, and you shall never see my face again."

"How can I give you his freedom since you threaten me?"

"That is easily done—there are pens and ink; a line from your Majesty——"

"Which you will carry to the prisoner."

"Nay, but which my servant shall carry."

"Your servant! You are not alone, then."

"The servants of Jesus are never alone, sire."

"And if I pardon this man—what then?"

"Your clemency for my mistress, Gabrielle de Vernet."

"What—you are a friend to Huguenots?"

"I am a friend to Huguenots such as she is."

"*Dieu, mon ami*, you risk much for your friends."

"What matter, since I befriend them. Your Majesty will sign the paper."

Louis took the pen in his hand. He trembled no longer. He was thinking that when the door was opened, he would cry for help. Once he had made his voice heard, he would have this priest flayed alive. Never should such a vengeance have been known. The idea pleased him. He wrote a few lines upon the paper, and handed them to Cavaignac.

"Well," said he, "bring me your messenger."

The priest read the paper through.

"Your Majesty has forgotten my mistress," said he.

"Ha! and what of her?"

"That she may leave the château immediately."

The king's hand trembled; he half raised it to strike the motionless figure before him. Then he remembered his idea, and wrote the order.

"Come," said he, "where is your servant?"

"He is here, sire."

The door of the inner room opened as the Jesuit spoke, and a man in the scarlet uniform of the musketeers saluted the "Well-Beloved." So sudden was his coming, that the king had not even time to rise from his chair before the door was shut again.

"See," said the priest, "the servants of Jesus are never alone, sire."

Louis stared at the musketeer as at an apparition.

"What!" said he, "a musketeer, too; by the mass, I am well served."

"Your Majesty sent for me," cried the trooper, saluting again.

"To carry this order for the release of the Lieutenant de Guyon, and for the horses of Madame de Vernet, who is leaving the château immediately," cried Cavaignac, as another oath sprang from the king's lips.

The trooper took the paper, to which the priest added three words of his own, and vanished as he had come.

"Well," said the king, "and what now?"

"That your Majesty will be pleased to sit until my mistress shall have reached the forest."

"That my arm may not reach her."

"Exactly, sire."

"And then—— ?"

"I shall have the honour to kiss your hand for the last time."

Louis laughed ironically.

"To-morrow, I shall settle with you," said he.

"As your Majesty wills."

The voice was the voice of a man who knew no emotions, of a man of iron. Yet could Louis have searched the heart of the Jesuit, courage would have rushed upon him like a freshet. Apprehension, racking fear, the thought of Gabrielle soon to lie in de Guyon's arms, an imagination depicting every phase of torture and of suffering that might be his—all these were contesting victory with the outward calm which the Jesuit displayed. Yet he did not move a hand while minutes passed; the great clock of the château struck nine, and still he stood like some ghostly shape of the night.

As the hour struck, the king, who had warred long with his passion, found himself able to subdue it no longer. Determined that he would stake all upon the hazard, he sprang of a sudden from his chair and ran to the window of the room. The court without echoed his alarm; the whole palace seemed to awake from sleep. Armed men burst into the room where the Jesuit had been; attendants, officials, valets pressed one upon another in the gallery.

" The priest—the priest—death to the assassin—seize the priest !"

A hundred voices took up the cry. It rang through court and cloister. It seemed to fill the palace.

But when the search was made, there was no man that could put hands upon the Jesuit.

He had vanished like a phantom.

CHAPTER XV.

EXODUS.

JUNE was waxing old, and the ripeness of the summer was upon the brown-burnt forest. Pools had become pits for lack of the rains ; rich grasses and rare blossoms were to be gathered in their beds. The sward had lost its green, and the shimmer of the relaxing heat searched meadows and glens alike. Even the streams flowed drowsily, and the deer herded in the cool of the dormant glades. Night had no gift of her breezes ; dawn no freshness of her sleep. The woodlanders dreamed through the long days ; desolation had come down upon the hamlets.

Towards the hour of sunset on the last Sunday of the month, Père Cavaignac stood upon a spur of the hill-

land above the Château aux Loups.
The kine in the meadows were then
turning to the water, there was a
certain awakening of brute life in all
the park about the château. But
while it was the hour for vespers and
for the coming of village folk, the
voice of man was not to be heard. A
great silence reigned in all the gardens of the house. No smoke rose
from its chimneys ; the gates of the
courtyard were shut ; the bells in the
tower no longer called to prayer ; the
name of its mistress was a word for
whispers in all the country round.
The home of " the little Huguenot"
was a home to her no more. She had
gone out of the lives of the people
like a sun that had set. And no man
was so bold that he lifted his voice to
mourn for her.

The priest stood in the shelter of
the thicket and looked down to the
belt of trees girdling about the château. There were moments when he
thought that he saw the flash of scarlet against the riper green of the

avenues ; other moments when he heard the blast of a horn and beheld a musketeer riding forth from the gates. The man struck the highway to Paris, and was lost quickly in a cloud of powdering dust. Then the desolation was supreme once more ; and all the gardens seemed to sleep.

Though it was plain that nothing was to be observed from the place upon the hill's brow, the Jesuit continued at his post until the church bells in the distant village were chiming eight, and the dusk had come down more plenteously. He appeared to be awaiting some turn of events at the château ; and when the half of an hour had passed, he was justified. Again the gates of the courtyard were opened ; again a horseman rode forth. He was Pepin, the guide, and at his heels there followed the Abbé Gondy upon his mule, and the old servant, Dominique, upon his feet, leading another mule that carried the baggage. In this order the little cavalcade struck the hill-path, and came on towards that very thicket in which the priest was watching.

It was near to being dark when at last the three arrived at the hill road. A gloomier company never set foot in the forest, nor one so melancholy. Gone was the fat from the cheeks of the Abbé, gone was the smile from the face of Pepin. The old servant walked with downcast eyes and trembling lips. He looked back often at the home he loved—it was no home to him now. He remembered that every brick of it, every path, every tree, every glade was like a friend to be lost. And never again would he behold them.

" Saints and angels defend us !" cried the Abbé as his mule entered the glade of the woods ; but Pepin said—

" Blood of Bartholomew ! there's a man that lurks amid the trees. He has eyes for your pack, my father."

" Little has the good God left to me," said the Abbé mournfully. " Have you your cudgel ready ?"

"Aye, surely, I have. But by the mass, Monsieur l'Abbé, I would sooner sing a dirge than cross a blade this night. Body of Paul! I have the plague at my knees."

"Wouldst that thou had it at thy throat for a brawling rogue," muttered the Abbé.

They rode for a space into the heart of the wood, and the figure in the thicket vanished as it had come.

But at the cross of the path it appeared again, and stood out in the waning light.

"*Gratias agamus!*" exclaimed the Abbé, "it is no robber, but my friend Cavaignac. Oh, blessed be God that he has come!"

"What," cried Pepin, "the dog of a Jesuit! Do you not know, my father, there are a thousand gold pieces upon his head?"

"Fool," said the Abbé, "would you hang from yonder tree?"

"It is thou that art the fool, wanting the courage of a hen," muttered Pepin, between his teeth; but when the Jesuit came up to them, he cried to him for a blessing.

Cavaignac had few words to utter, and those he spoke quickly.

" So you leave the château, my friend," said he to the Abbé.

" How! You have not heard? The king's musketeers sleep in our house like swine. Oh, cursed day that has robbed me of board and bed!"

The Jesuit looked at him with hard contempt.

" And madame—— ?" he asked.

" Has crossed the Rhine," said the old man Dominique. " *Dieu*, what a night that was! Is there one that rides as she rides? Surely it was her courage that saved him from the king's men like a deer dragged from the dogs. And now she is with him where no king may harm her. Blessed be the God she served!"

For a spell the Jesuit was silent. When he spoke again, it was to the Abbé.

" Whither go you now?" he asked.

" Aye, whither go we now ?" chimed in Pepin ; " to the devil, so it would appear."

" If, perchance, you could lead me to any shelter," stammered the Abbé, " to any house of your holy Order where I can be sure of a cup of wine and a dish of meat, with what thanks will my heart be filled ! Well am I punished for my sins. But the good God may yet permit me to repent. Oh, that I should have no pillow for my head, no drink for my lips ! You pity me, my friend ?"

" Nay," said the Jesuit suddenly, " why should I pity you ? Are you weary, then take a pillow of the grass ; do you thirst, there is the stream for your lips ; if you hunger, gather fruit as you go. But, above all things, give thanks to God in that he has permitted you still to sleep, still to thirst, still to hunger."

He turned away with the words and the night hid him from their view.

" Surely the man has a devil," said the Abbé.